The (Im)Perfect Church

Studies in I Corinthians

Rubel Shelly

20th Century Christian
2809 Granny White Pike
Nashville, Tennessee 37204

To Myra

Table of Contents

Preface vii

1/ Paul and Corinth 1

2/ A Divided Church 11

3/ How Do You View the Gospel? 19

4/ The Apostolic Ministry 29

5/ The Leaven of Sin in a Church 41

6/ Transformed People and Their Obligations. . 51

7/ Counsel About Marriage 63

8/ Freedom: Its Reality and Limits 77

9/ Respecting God's Order of Things 91

10/ Spiritual Gifts in the Early Church 103

11/ Must We Believe in the Resurrection? 117

12/ A Final Word – And Farewell 131

Preface

My two sons and I sometimes ride dirt bikes together. One day a terrible thunderstorm forced us to take shelter. We huddled together in a dirty construction site under a just-started structure. The ground was muddy, the water leaked on our heads, and we were anything but comfortable. If it had not been for the storm, we would never have chosen to spend any time there.

The church at Corinth was not the sort of place most of us would choose for the nurturing of our spiritual lives. Had it not been for the terrible atmosphere of the city itself, the seeking of spiritual shelter in that just-begun body of believers might have been unthinkable.

In fact, given the warts and flaws of the churches you and I know, we might not think them such desirable places to be – until we focus on what is happening on the outside of those bodies. The storm of sin rages and destroys. Rains fall, winds blow, and floods beat against us. So we seek shelter in places which have a firm footing on the Word of God – even though the total structure may yet be unfinished and rough.

The body of Christ in Corinth was *not* a perfect church. In his *Essays on Paul,* C. K. Barrett observes that the Corinthian epistles provide "the most complete and many-sided picture" of how the great Apostle to the Gentiles believed the gospel was to be expressed in the life of a church. He says: "To say this is not to claim that the Corinthian church was a paragon of all churches; there was often a wide divergence between what happened in Corinth and what Paul thought ought to happen" (p. 1). The same is often true in the church of God today.

We know the New Testament ideal; we are frustrated by our practical failures to measure up to that ideal. First Corinthians provides insights and encouragements for our present-day struggle.

Authors cited in various parts of this book are listed in the bibliography at the end. Unless actual page numbers are identified, the reference is to the discussion in that author's work of the verse(s) under consideration in this volume. Primary Scripture quotations are from the American Standard Version (1901) unless otherwise noted.

I hope you enjoy using this book as a stimulus to the study of one of the most fascinating of all the New Testament epistles.

Rubel Shelly

The (Im)Perfect Church

1/ Paul and Corinth

1 Cor. 1:1-9; Acts 18:1-17

As you study Paul's first letter to the church at Corinth, mixed emotions will stir within your heart; you will have occasion both to rejoice and lament. As Paul traces the wisdom of God in the gospel of the cross and the beauty of Christian life and service, your heart will thrill with joy. As you learn of the carnal hearts and wicked lives of many of the Christians at Corinth, your heart will sink in despair.

It is imperative that Christians today study this epistle deeply and reverently, however, for the same contrast between *divine ideal* and *human perform-ance* which was evident at Corinth is still the realistic life situation of God's people on earth.

We need the ideal held before our eyes for the sake of understanding and motivation in spiritual things. We need to evaluate ourselves honestly in light of that ideal and grow by divine grace into the likeness of Christ. We need to remember and appreciate the magnificence of our Savior's patience with us in our weaknesses.

A Troubled Church

The church at Corinth had problems! Division, immoral conduct, brethren fighting one another in the courts, marriage and divorce controversies, abuses of the Lord's Supper, etc. The list just goes on and on. *But Paul hadn't given up on that church.* While some of us might have written off the whole bunch and said that God had no people at Corinth, the apostle still regarded that troubled body as "the church of God which is at Corinth" (1:2; cf. 2 Cor. 1:1).

What do we do when there are church troubles? Grumble. Run from them by moving on to another church. Pull off and start a new congregation – which has no fellowship with the old one. Maybe just "drop out" altogether and excuse it on the basis of all the turmoil in the church.

Paul reacted differently. He was determined to do everything within his power to help resolve the problems, restore unity, and see that none perished! We can learn a great deal from his approach and his inspired counsel.

Some Data on Corinth

Located on a narrow strip of land connecting Northern Greece with the Peloponnesus, Corinth was a thriving center for travel and trade in the first-century world. It controlled north-south commerce by virtue of its strategic location. Difficult sailing around the Peloponnesus gave Corinth command even over east-west traffic between Rome and the Near East; it was safer to transport cargo overland at Corinth between its port cities of Cenchrea on the east and Lechaeum on the west than to run the risk of navigating harsh seas. An ingenious system used rollers and slave labor to drag cargo overland for approximately four miles from one port to the other.

The city was enormously wealthy – with the liabilities as well as assets which attend such prosperity. A pleasure-mad and immoral atmosphere had been cultivated over the years. Corinth came to be what one historian described as "the cesspool of the ancient world." Drunkenness, prostitution, brawling, murder, and the other things one might associate with a "wild city" were all in evidence there.

Corinth was the capital city of the province of Achaia when Paul wrote this epistle. Its population was something near a half-million souls.

What religion there was at Corinth centered around the polytheistic gods of Greco-Roman mythology. In particular, the worship of Aphrodite – the Greek "goddess of love" – had a large following at Corinth. Instead of moderating the evils of the city, however, the Aphrodite cult only contributed to it. The priestesses of the cult were "sacred prostitutes," and the worship center was nothing more than a brothel. Madvig writes of the city:

> The most conspicuous landmark at Corinth was the Acrocorinth, a mountain to the south of the city. Reaching a height of 1886 ft. (575 m.), it was an ideal situation for a fortress that could control all the trade routes into the Peloponnesus. The temple of Aphrodite, the goddess of love and beauty, stood on its highest peak. The thousand female prostitutes who served there contributed to Corinth's reputation for immorality. In fact, it is to this evil trade carried on in the name of religion that Strabo, the geographer, ascribed the prosperity of the city. The degree to which Corinth was given over to vice is apparent as early as the time of Aristophanes by the coining of the word *korinthia-*

zomai (lit. "Corinthianize"), meaning "practice immorality"; similarly "Corinthian girl" (Gk. *Korinthia korē*) designated a prostitute. That the situation continued into Paul's day is evidenced by the evils he attacks in his Corinthian letters.

Background to the Letter

Few elderships or Missions Committees would have selected such a city as a promising site for an evangelistic campaign. But Corinth is precisely where the Holy Spirit led Paul on his second missionary journey.

Paul arrived at Corinth from Athens in early A.D. 50 (Acts 18:1). There he ran into two Jewish believers recently arrived from Rome, Aquila and Priscilla. He lived with them and joined them in working at their common trade as tentmakers (i.e., canvass workers) to support himself (Acts 18:2-3).

The great apostle was preaching the gospel to all who would listen. Every sabbath in the synagogue, he "reasoned" and "persuaded Jews and Greeks" that Jesus was the Christ (Acts 18:4). Joined later by Silas and Timothy, his ministry had tremendous success. It was so successful, in fact, that the Jewish leaders rose up against him and blasphemed Jesus (Acts 18:5-6).

His work continued from the base of the house of Titus Justus, likely one of the several "God-fearers" (i.e., Gentiles who revered the God of the Jews without becoming formal proselytes) the apostle encountered in his journeys (Acts 18:7). Even the ruler of the Corinthian synagogue and his family were converted to Christ (Acts 18:8a). "Many of the Corinthians hearing believed, and were baptized" (Acts 18:8b).

Paul stayed in Corinth for a total of eighteen months to teach the Word of God in that city and to help establish the church in such a hostile environment (Acts 18:9-11).

In late 51 or early 52, he decided to move on to Ephesus (Acts 18:12-21). There he stayed for three years (Acts 19; cf. 20:31).

During the extended ministry at Ephesus, Paul naturally was concerned to know the situation of the young body of believers he had established at Corinth. When word came to him of immorality in the church, he wrote them a letter and gave counsel about dealing with the problem (1 Cor. 5:9ff). This epistle was written prior to the one we call 1 Corinthians and is not preserved to us.

The letter we call 1 Corinthians is therefore his *second* written communication with the saints at Corinth. [Note: Second Corinthians is in reality Paul's *fourth* letter to Corinth, for between his two preserved epistles to the Corinthians was a "letter of tears" referred to in 2 Cor. 2:3-4.]

Since Paul left Ephesus in the spring of A.D. 55, we are able to date the epistle we are studying with some degree of certainty. From 1 Cor. 16:8, we know the apostle was still at Ephesus and planning to leave around the time of Jewish Pentecost (i.e., late May or early June) when he wrote the epistle. Thus we shall assign the date of *early A.D. 55* to the book we are studying.

It addresses a situation which was deteriorating rapidly. The immorality about which he had written already was not only unresolved but was now even worse. And the church had responded to Paul's letter with one of its own – containing a list of questions concerning which they needed guidance (1 Cor. 7:1). Add to that the report brought to him by the people from Chloe's household (1:11) and the apostle's concern must have been tremendous.

Thus he wrote the epistle we call 1 Corinthians and developed the theme *righteous living as the people of God* at great length. He called on his brothers and sisters at wicked Corinth to live up to their status in Christ rather than fall back to the sorry level of their pre-conversion life.

Paul's Love for the Corinthians

Was Paul grieved by the problems at Corinth? Of course. Was he concerned that some there were in jeopardy for their souls? Certainly. Did doctrinal error threaten the church's identity in that pagan city? Yes.

So how did he begin his letter? With anathemas, condemnations, rebukes, and threats? No – though that is often *our* approach to troubled churches or sinning individuals.

Changing Their Self-Image (1:1-3)

He opened the letter with a *series of affirmations* about his readers.

With all their problems, they were still the people of God! They were still "the church of God which is at Corinth" (1:2a). They were "sanctified in Christ Jesus" (1:2b). They were "saints" (1:2c). Paul would never abandon this positive view of the troubled Corinthian church in his letter to it. He will later call them "brethren" (1:10; 2:1; 3:1, *et al*.), "God's husbandry, God's building" (3:9), "a temple of God" (3:16), etc.

Have you ever noticed how children tend to live up to the names you give them? Call one "clumsy," and he probably will be; call her "poor in math," and she probably will be. On the other hand, call her "thoughtful," and she likely will be a thoughtful person; call him "a good student," and he will more nearly hit the books like a true scholar.

Self-image is important. It becomes something of a self-fulfilling prophecy to see yourself as worthwhile or worthless. If Paul could foster a positive image of the spiritual status of these people, he would be in better position to call on them to live differently.

Paul and Sosthenes (cf. Acts 18:17) joined to greet this church and to wish it "grace" and "peace" (1:3) –not fire and brimstone! –from heaven.

Thanksgiving For The Corinthians (1:4-9)

Then, believe it or not, Paul proceeded to relate the gist of his constant prayers of *thanksgiving* on their behalf.

This paragraph seems to have particular reference to the spiritual gifts which Paul knew to be present among the Corinthians (cf. 1 Cor. 12-14). Their presence was proof to Paul that these people had indeed been recipients of God's grace (1:4-5). Their conversion to the Lord had not been mere pretence or hypocrisy. Although men cannot know hearts, heaven can. That God would send spiritual gifts among them was clear evidence that they had been genuinely converted and were receiving confirmation of their faith through such gifts (1:6-7).

The apostle knew that the presence of the Holy Spirit in their midst gave hope for victory over their various problems. After all, the primary purpose of the giving of the Spirit never has been to impart miraculous powers but to enable the people of God for their struggle with sin. Believers who draw close to the Father will be "strengthened with power through his Spirit in the inward man" (Eph. 3:16). In the sixth chapter of this epistle to the saints at Corinth, Paul will appeal to the fact of the Spirit's presence in them as a motivation to moral purity.

No, he was not ready to give up on the church he had founded at Corinth. He knew that it was possible for his work among them to be in vain, but he was far from ready to concede the point. The same divine power that could turn a Jewish persecutor of Christians into a missionary could transform pagans into people reflecting the very glory of God in their wicked city!

Paul's confidence was not so much in the Corinthians as in the God whose grace had been evidenced among them. Thus the opening verses of the letter are less a pep talk along you-can-do-better lines than a positive assurance that divine power was still among them. "God is faithful" (1:9a) – even when you're not. The one who called you "into the fellowship of his Son" (1:9b) still wants you to maintain that relationship – even though you are struggling right now. God is not anxious to quit on you but to "confirm you unto the end" (1:8a) and to present you "unreprovable in the day of our Lord Jesus Christ" (1:8b).

In order for God to finish the work of redemption he had begun at Corinth, some things had to have immediate attention!

Conclusion

Corinth was hardly an ideal or perfect church. It had more problems than any other church I have ever seen or heard about. Yet that body of struggling, carnal, and imperfect people was God's church in that city.

Thank God for his patience with his people. Thank God for people such as Paul who will step in and help rather than avoid troubled churches. And thank God for faithful Christians who will stay, work through problems, and rescue a church from ruin.

Know any less-than-perfect churches today? If so, this letter may have something to say which will be of real value to you.

Study Questions

1. What are some typical reactions to "church troubles" today? How do these reactions compare with Paul's reaction to the host of problems at Corinth?

2. Summarize the information given in this chapter (and in additional reading from Bible dictionaries, commentaries, etc.) about the city of Corinth. With what modern city might it be compared for size and commercial activity?

3. What were the primary religious cults and influences at Corinth?

4. From a careful reading of Acts 18, reconstruct the beginnings of the church at Corinth. What caused Paul to choose Corinth? What would have been the primary obstacles to his work? What would have been his primary opportunities?

5. How many letters did Paul write to the church at Corinth? How does our epistle of 1 Corinthians fit into the sequence?

6. What is the *theme* of this epistle? From your preliminary acquaintance with the letter, how do you see Paul going about the development of that theme?

7. How does Paul's approach to the troubled church at Corinth differ from the one preachers and writers sometimes use today in approaching similar situations?

8. Give some serious thought to the matter of *self-image* in the lives of individuals and churches. How can a positive self-image affect a person or congregation? What about a negative one?

9. What was the basis for Paul's *thanksgiving* for the saints at Corinth?

10. Given the situation of the church at Corinth and the purpose of 1 Corinthians, what potential value do you see for your study of this book?

2/ A Divided Church

1 Cor. 1:10-17; 3:1-23

Given all the problems at Corinth, where would one begin in trying to deal with them?

There is no more serious or heart-rending problem dealt with in the Corinthian correspondence than the very first one mentioned. There were *divisions among brethren* at Corinth.

When the Holy Spirit moved Paul to write this epistle, he led him to face the problem of the party spirit first. This can hardly be coincidental. If this problem were not resolved, most of the others to be discussed in the letter could never be dealt with effectively. For example, how could the church at Corinth discipline the brazenly immoral person of chapter five except through a united action?

Fragmenting the Body

If any situation among the people of Christ's church is sad enough to make angels weep, it is this one. Division (Gk, *schisma*) makes the church vulnerable before Satan and the world. The new life in Christ is meant to be lived in unity and peace among brethren (John 17:20-21).

The Appeal (1:10)

Paul's approach to the divisions at Corinth was not that of a threatening parent with a rod; it was that of a loving brother and concerned teacher. He called on the various groups to come together as one. "Now I beseech you, brethren, through the name of our Lord Jesus Christ, that ye all speak the same thing, and that there be no divisions among you; but that ye be perfected together in the same mind and in the same judgment."

When forces emerge within a church which create dissension and quarreling, the body is in real danger. The pettier the issue capable of creating friction, the greater the danger.

The apostle wanted the church to "be perfected together" rather than pulling against itself. The Greek word (katartizō) means to put in order, make complete, or mend. It is used in Mark 1:19 of mending fishing nets and in nonbiblical literature of knitting broken bones back together. Division within the church is unnatural, painful, and wrong. It must not go unattended.

The Corinthian Factions (1:11-12)

Ironically, the contentions within the body at Corinth were centered around personalities and ministries(1:12). How typical! The things which divide churches today are seldom "doctrinal issues" so much as personal loyalties. An elder doesn't get his way, a preacher is asked to leave, some members are miffed that the location they favored for the new church building is not chosen – and the church chooses up sides, has a nasty fuss, and splits. The church is a spectacle before the world, and weak Christians fall away from the faith.

There had been no conscious fostering of contentions among the various evangelists who had labored at Corinth. Paul and Apollos had not worked against one another; Peter was probably known there only by name and reputation. They had no contentions among themselves. They were not promoting personal allegiances among the Corinthians.

It is pointless to speculate concerning the differences of teaching which were characteristic of the four groups. Paul is not concerned so much with their peculiar tenets as with their mere existence. It was the *party spirit* being demonstrated which was the primary problem. The injection of a divisive spirit into the body of Christ is wrong (cf. Gal. 5:20).

Paul's Opening Argument (1:13-17)

The apostle's first argument against the party spirit at Corinth led him to remind the brethren there of their conversion and baptism. "Is Christ divided? Was Paul crucified for you? Or were ye baptized into the name of Paul? I thank God that I baptized none of you, save Crispus and Gaius; lest any man should say that ye were baptized into my name. And I baptized also the household of Stephanas: besides, I know not whether I baptized any other" (1:13-16).

Some have used this passage to disparage baptism. To the contrary. It does not depreciate baptism but indicates that some of the Corinthians had failed to understand its significance.

Baptism does not bind one to the preacher who performs the physical act of immersing (1:15c). New Testament baptism is "in the name of Jesus Christ" (Acts 2:38; 8:16; 10:48, *et al.*) and binds the one being immersed to Jesus as Savior and Lord.

Paul seems to have been aware of the possibility of personality cults emerging within the church even before this Corinthian problem arose. Thus it was his deliberate custom to avoid preaching in a style that would call attention to himself (i.e., "not in wisdom of words," 1:17b); he seems also to have left the baptizing of his converts to his working associates (1:17a).

Paul's mission was to preach the gospel. Silas and Timothy (Acts 18:5) or his first converts at Corinth could attend to the baptisms (cf. Acts 18:8). Too much attention to preachers and too little to Christ was voiding the cross of its power.

A Right View of Preachers

Perhaps there has always been a tendency for people to misunderstand the role of preachers of the gospel. Some evangelists evidently desire the "chief seats" in the church; thus the modern pastor system has emerged. Some preachers are "put on pedestals" against their wills; this was surely the case of Paul, Cephas, and Apollos.

Most preachers see themselves as Christian servants with a particular function to perform for the benefit of the body. They regard each other as co-workers instead of competitors. They seek no personal glory for themselves and ask no personal following.

A Second Argument (3:1-15)

Thus Paul's second argument against division at Corinth is built around a right view of preachers. The entire third chapter of the book is devoted to it.

Partyism and quarreling at Corinth proved the believers there were still largely "babes" and "carnal" (3:1-3). Why? Strife around human leaders is hardly an activity of spiritual maturity (3:4); to the contrary, such a spirit is among the "works of the flesh" (cf. Gal. 5:20). Surely it grieved Paul to have to speak so harshly to his spiritual charges.

Yet their situation was not one which allowed subtle hints. The point had to be made, and he had to have their attention for the hearing of it.

Paul had founded the church at Corinth (3:6a). Apollos had followed him there (3:6b; cf. Acts 18:24-28). The process was a natural one, and there was no competition between the two men. Both men were merely servants in the vineyard of God (3:7-9). One planted; one watered; God gave the increase (3:6c). Neither man had sought personal recognition or loyalty for his service to deity. It was the carnality of the Corinthians that had caused some of them to take the names of Paul and Apollos as rallying cries. We have no idea how the name of Cephas (i.e., Peter) got into the contest. Worst of all was the fact that some were even using the name of Christ in a divisive way.

Paul's approach was not to side with one party against the other three. Instead, recognizing all four parties collectively as the "church of God at Corinth" (cf. 1:2), he appealed for them to drop their partyism for the sake of unity. The building is God's; the foundation is Christ himself (3:10-11); Paul, Apollos, and Cephas were workers building to the glory of God on that foundation (3:12-15).

A Solemn Warning (3:16-17)

Did the Corinthians understand? Had the point been made with adequate force? Lest anyone should miss it, a beautiful fact and a solemn warning are joined in one statement.

"Know ye not that ye are a temple of God, and that the Spirit of God dwelleth in you? If any man destroyeth the temple of God, him shall God destroy; for the temple of God is holy, and such are ye" (3:16-17).

Paul will later refer to individual bodies of Christians as dwelling places of the Spirit of God in connection with an argument against sexual impurity (1 Cor. 6:19). His point here is very different, however. His reference is not to individual believers but to the collective body of Christians at Corinth.

The church is God's *temple* by virtue of the Spirit's presence within it. The figure is a beautiful one. The church is the locus of God's presence with mankind, for that is what the Old Testament temple signified.

The universal body of Christ on earth cannot be destroyed (cf. Matt. 16:18). But local churches can destroy themselves and pass out of existence through false teaching (cf. Rev. 2:5; 3:16) or factious behavior. The church at Corinth was in danger and needed to appreciate that fact.

Playing By The World's Rules (3:18-23)

What was happening at Corinth is what has happened to countless churches since that time. The church is supposed to be in the world but not of the world. It doesn't always work that way. Sometimes the church is not only in the world but brings the world's ways into the church. It will not work. A boat in the lake is one thing; the lake in the boat is another. It sinks!

The church at Corinth had brought too much of the world into itself. It was playing by the rules of worldly competition in a spiritual body which needed a different spirit altogether.

Worldly wisdom calls for self-exaltation (3:18) and caters to pride in the teacher's rhetoric and style. The wisdom of God is wholly different (3:19-23). It has its power in the message itself (cf. Rom. 1:16) and not the messenger. "Wherefore let no one glory in men" (3:21a).

Conclusion

That Christ is not divided (literally, "broken into pieces," 1:13a) is a lesson not yet appreciated or learned. The Lord wants one fold with one shepherd (John 10:16). Division of that fold grieves the Savior and weakens the body.

It is true that God's faithful people must separate themselves from certain people or groups (cf. 2 John 9-11), yet many – if not most – of the divisions in the body of Christ are like those at Corinth. They owe their origin to carnal hearts and worldly wisdom.

God's people must seek peace with one another (Rom. 14:19). We must refuse to be contentious and quarrelsome (2 Tim. 2:24-26). And in cases of offenses among brethren, we must seek reconciliation according to the Lord's will (Eph. 4:32; cf. Matt. 18:15-17).

The Lord died *to bring all men together in one body. May we* live *for that same goal!*

Study Questions

1. Why was the problem of division in the Corinthian church treated first? What implications did this issue have for the other things which needed attention there?

2. The focal point of the divisions at Corinth was personal loyalty to preachers. Why does this same pattern seem to perpetuate itself through history?

3. What do you know of the history of Paul, Apollos, and Cephas in relation to the church at Corinth? Why would their names have surfaced as the rallying points for the different parties?

4. Summarize Paul's first argument against the divisions at Corinth.

5. What are some of the typical misunderstandings which still exist concerning the role of gospel preachers? Where does the responsibility lie for these misunderstandings?

6. Summarize Paul's second argument against the divisions at Corinth.

7. How did Christ's name enter into the controversy among the various parties? Can even the divine name be used in a divisive and carnal manner?

8. Develop Paul's point made in 1 Corinthians 3:12-15. Do some research on this passage in order to interpret it correctly. What are some of its implications for our work for Christ?

9. What is the point of calling the church God's *temple*? How does this relate to the subject of division?

10. Contrast the wisdom of the world and the wisdom of God. What was Paul's point in bringing up the topic? How does it relate to the party spirit at Corinth?

3/ How Do You View the Gospel?

1 Cor. 1:18–2:16

The origin of much of the division in the history of the church has been pride in men and their accomplishments. I have a favorite preacher; you have a favorite preacher. I have a ministry to perform; you have a ministry to perform. Let our egos get on the line, and we may sever fellowship with one another and divide the church over those preferences and good works!

Isn't that what was going on at Corinth? Different people in that body were proud of certain preachers, and they boasted of certain spiritual gifts they had (cf. 1 Cor. 12-14). The result was division.

In the previous chapter, we saw how Paul rebuked the party spirit at Corinth and explained the complementary role of preachers. The ultimate remedy to division rooted in pride is *a proper appreciation of the gospel of Christ*. Preaching a crucified Christ does not minister to pride, arrogance, and division. It demolishes them all and binds men together in humble submission to the one who humbled himself to suffer for us.

Divine "Foolishness"

There is nothing about the message of Christ or the church which wears his name which is constituted as a ministry to pride. In the eyes of the world, the gospel message is "foolishness" and the church is "despised."

Paul appeals to these facts as an implicit rebuke to the snobbery which was creating divisions at Corinth.

A "Foolish" Gospel (1:18-25)

Heaven did not provide a Savior in the way men were expecting. The Jews had wanted a spectacular display of power (1:22a), for they wanted a Messiah who would restore them to the glory days of David and Solomon. The Greeks wanted philosophical speculation in the tradition of Plato or Aristotle (1:22b), for they believed salvation would come to men through knowledge and special insights for the initiated.

Neither the Jewish nor Greek expectation had any place for a lowly man whose career ended with a horrible death which was reserved for the worst of criminals. "For the word of the cross is to them that perish foolishness; but unto us who are saved it is the power of God" (1:18; cf. 1:23-24).

Human wisdom (i.e., knowledge and skill divorced from God) has been productive in history – but usually of harm instead of benefit. It has created strife, hatred, and weapons of war; it has sought wealth, fame, and fortune; it has exalted man over his Creator and set him against his fellow man. No wonder, then, that God has determined to "destroy the wisdom of the wise" (1:19a) and has "made foolish the wisdom of the world" (1:20c) through Jesus.

None of this is to say that the gospel message is one of mysticism or irrationality. It is simply to say that it did not originate with, does not depend on, and ought never to be used to foster pride in human accomplishment.

There is no "human accomplishment" with the gospel. It is a message of divine ministry through grace to sinful humans. We were lost and could not save ourselves. God acted through Jesus Christ to save us by his once-for-all sacrifice of himself as the Lamb of God who takes away sin (cf. John 1:29; Heb. 10:1-10). We are saved by grace through faith and not by our good works which would justify pride (Eph. 2:8-9).

The message of a crucified Savior may be "foolishness" to Gentiles and a "stumbling block" to Jews (1:22-23), "but unto them that are called, both Jews and Greeks, Christ the power of God, and the wisdom of God" (1:24).

A "Despised" Church (1:26-29)

As surely as the cross is a source of humility rather than pride, so does the church fail to minister to human pride.

The church at Corinth had few wise, mighty, or noble people (1:26-29). To the contrary, most of them were common people. Before their conversion, they had been thieves, harlots, alcoholics, and homosexuals! There was nothing about the church to justify the divisions they were fostering.

One insult hurled at the church from the earliest days of her existence has been the rag-tag nature of her membership. Celsus was a bitter second-century opponent of Christianity. In his work *True Discourse,* he attacked Jesus as the illegitimate son of a poor woman and Christianity as the religion of vulgar and ignorant people. As quoted by Origen, he said this of Christians: "Their commandments are like this. 'Let no one educated, no one wise, no one sensible draw near. For these abilities are thought by us to be evils. But as for anyone ignorant, anyone stupid, anyone uneducated, anyone who is a child, let him come boldly.' By the fact that they themselves admit that these people are worthy of their god, they show that they want and are able to convince only the foolish, dishonorable and stupid, and only slaves, women, and little children" (*Against Celsus* 3. 44.).

On Celsus' view of the matter, Christianity's appeal to the lower classes was proof of its falsehood. On Paul's view of the matter, its appeal to the outcasts and dregs of society demonstrated God's love and showed that he did not judge men and women by externals (e.g., wealth) but by their hearts (e.g., penitence over sin). On either view of the matter, there is nothing about the church which promotes pride in human status and accomplishment.

The wealthy and pseudo-sophisticated may feel sufficient of themselves; the humble and penitent seek their sufficiency in Christ. Christians have accepted Jesus Christ as their only hope and refuse to boast in themselves. Our confidence is in him alone.

Paul's Preaching

Paul reminded the Corinthians again (cf. 1:14-17) of his personal ministry of the gospel among them. There is hardly a more moving passage in all the apostle's letters than this. It shows the heart of the man who had turned from persecutor to missionary.

The Manner (2:1-3)

His method of preaching at Corinth – as everywhere else – was designed not to call attention to himself or to promote personal loyalties. He employed no empty rhetoric (i.e., "excellency of speech") or cleverness (i.e., "wisdom") with which to lead his hearers into something they would later regret (2:1). The modern imagery might be to say that Paul did not "sell" his gospel at Corinth with the manipulative techniques of an unscrupulous used-car salesman.

He exalted Jesus. He preached the cross (2:2). He explained the divine solution to the sin problem. He took seriously the words of Jesus about the death on Calvary: "And I, if I be lifted up from the earth, will draw all men unto myself" (John 12:32).

Some have supposed the "weakness," "fear," and "much trembling" Paul mentioned here (2:3) refer to his sense of defeat over his ministry at Athens. That would be strange indeed! From reading Acts 17:16-34, one would hardly get the sense that his work there was a failure. It is much more reasonable and suits the context much better to see these words as descriptions of Paul's sense of unworthiness to be preaching such a wonderful message. It is the sense of inadequacy for the task which every faithful preacher of the gospel feels when he attempts to present the greatest story ever told.

The Motive (2:4-5)

Paul's motive for preaching the way he did was the noblest possible: he wanted the faith of his hearers to stand in the power of God and not in the wisdom of men.

Some of the evangelistic methods which people have tried in modern times give cause for alarm. They appear centered on charismatic individuals rather than Christ; they seem to be thinly veiled fund-raising efforts rather than ministries of truth. The "conversions" produced under such ministries must be sustained in some artificial manner by keeping a group very tightly knit in some type of cultic allegiance.

The right method will be used only when the right motive is behind the effort.

About a year after writing this epistle, Paul wrote a letter to the church at Rome. There is even good reason for thinking he may have been at Corinth at the time of his writing of Romans. At any rate, he addressed the topic of persons causing "divisions" within the church. He wrote of such persons: "For they that are such serve not our Lord Christ, but their own belly; and by their smooth and fair speech they beguile the hearts of the innocent" (Rom. 16:17-18). His own example with the gospel stood in sharp contrast with those who, whether at Corinth or Rome, would use the gospel in a self-seeking way and generate divisions thereby.

The Spirit's Ministry

The simple and unpretentious preaching of the apostle at Corinth had resulted in redemption and transformation for many. This confirmed that the power of the gospel was not in the eloquence or form of its presentation but in its content alone. The good news of Christ is God's power to save all people – even when preached by people lacking in worldly wisdom and eloquence.

The message of Christ is revealed from God through the Holy Spirit and owes nothing to human wisdom.

True Wisdom (2:6-11)

Having spoken of a pretentious wisdom of this world in a disparaging way, Paul now turns to speak of wisdom in a good sense. If there is a "wisdom of this world" which "none of the rulers of this world hath known," there is also a "wisdom not of this world" (i.e., "God's wisdom in a mystery") which has been freely given to all who will receive it (2:7-8).

When the word "mystery" (Gk, *mysterion*) is used in the New Testament, it refers to something which was once hidden from view but is now revealed. God's mystery, which constitutes the "wisdom not of this world" (2:6), is not something different from the gospel Paul has been discussing already. It is simply another way of designating it.

In ages past, men may have speculated about divine deliverance – both Jews and Greeks. In their self-proclaimed "wisdom," they missed it (2:9). The marvelous things of salvation which men could not envision have been revealed to us by the Spirit of God. "But unto us God revealed them through the Spirit: for the Spirit searcheth all things, yea, the deep things of God" (2:10).

True wisdom, then, does not arise from Paul, Cephas, Apollos, or the Corinthians; it is derived by revelation from the Spirit of God (2:11). Revealed through apostles and prophets, it is received humbly and obediently by those who believe their Christ-centered message.

Spiritual Discernment (2:12-16)

These verses contain a marvelous affirmation concerning the gospel. Having just defined true wisdom, Paul now speaks of its origin. If it did not come through our human insights and worldly wisdom, whence did it come? The Holy Spirit of God is the source of the Christ-centered message Paul had preached at Corinth (2:12).

About the role of apostles and other specially chosen instruments of revelation, Paul wrote: "Which things also we speak, not in words which man's wisdom teacheth, but which the Spirit teacheth; combining spiritual things with spiritual words" (2:13). When men spoke from God, they were guided by his Spirit to the degree that even the words they used were certified correct. They spoke in their own vocabularies and styles, yet they spoke the words God wanted spoken in a given situation (cf. Matt. 10:19; 2 Pet. 1:21).

Paul consistently claimed to have the supernatural gift of prophecy (2:16) and expected people who heard him, saw the confirming signs he worked, and witnessed the fruit of his ministry to acknowledge that gift. "If any man thinketh himself to be a prophet or spiritual, let him take knowledge of the things which I write unto you, that they are the commandment of the Lord" (1 Cor. 14:37; cf. 1 Thess. 2:13).

Conclusion

There is a right way to view the gospel. Just as surely, there is a wrong way.

The wrong way is to see the gospel as a human attainment in which we may glory. It is not of human origin; it does not exalt men; it does not sponsor and encourage divisions among those who have embraced it.

The right way is to see it as a revelation from God through his Holy Spirit which has been delivered to us through specially chosen and faithful servants. Our loyalty is to the Christ who is at the heart of that gospel – not to the messengers bearing the word. Since we did not come to this gospel through our own strivings and human wisdom but by grace, we can only rejoice with believers who have accepted this same wonderful truth and stand together with them in one spiritual body.

Study Questions

1. This chapter begins with an assertion about the source of much of the division in church history. What is that assertion? Do you agree with it?

2. What is suggested as the "remedy" for divisions rooted in pride? React to that suggestion.

3. Discuss Ephesians 2:8-9 in relation to the issues raised in this chapter.

4. What was the background of the Christians at Corinth before their conversion? What should this have told those people about pride in themselves?

5. A quotation is given in the chapter from Celsus. Reflect on that quotation and the perspective it offers on the membership of the body of Christ. Are modern churches sometimes to careful about "our image" in the community?

6. Discuss Paul's comments about the manner of his ministry at Corinth. Did his educational background include training in style, rhetorical skills, and the like? What did he mean by his statement?

7. Identify the motive Paul said was behind his work. How did this keep his manner of preaching pure?

8. Paul discussed two kinds of wisdom in vs. 6-11. Distinguish them carefully.

9. The word "mystery" has a slightly different meaning in the New Testament than in some of its modern uses. Distinguish these meanings.

10. Discuss the implications of vs. 12-16 for the doctrine of inspiration. What do the words "verbal" and "plenary" mean when used in the context of discussing the inspiration of Scripture?

4/ The Apostolic Ministry

1 Cor. 4:1-21; 9:1-27

There is a natural curiosity on our part about the apostles of the Lord Jesus Christ. They were his most intimate associates. They were chosen to be with him to learn of the kingdom of God, given special authority to preach the gospel of the grace of God, and empowered with miraculous gifts by the Spirit of God (cf. Mark 3:14-15). Their self-sacrificing labors resulted in the establishment of the church throughout the civilized world of the first century.

To use Paul's language, the apostles served as Christ's "ambassadors" to the world. "We are ambassadors therefore on behalf of Christ, as though God were entreating by us: we beseech you on behalf of Christ, be ye reconciled to God" (2 Cor. 5:20). An ambassador of the United States is no ordinary citizen in Great Britain, China, or France; he has special authority to speak for the government, negotiate relationships, and make commitments. So did the apostles have unparalleled authority to speak for Christ and to bind and loose on earth what had been already settled in heaven (Matt. 18:18).

Because of the sense of awe we feel in relation to the Twelve and Paul, there has been a tendency to lose perspective on them and their work. They are often thought of as not quite human. Thus we speak of "Saint Matthew," "Saint Peter," and "Saint Paul"; these men become figures in stained glass windows who are accorded reverence due only the Lord Jesus himself. The danger of allowing healthy appreciation of such persons to degenerate into unhealthy adoration is evident at Corinth.

Who Were Those Men?

The apostles and prophets of the early church were ordinary men who became extraordinary through their total commitment to Christ. While they received their revelations and signs by supernatural means through the Holy Spirit, they had to develop their personal zeal for and devotion to that truth in the same way we do.

By understanding their ministry and observing their examples of personal service, we can be made bolder to serve the Lord acceptably in our generation. More godly zeal and devotion in us will allow the Word of God to have greater impact on our contemporaries (cf. Acts 17:6).

How They Regarded Themselves (4:1-7)

Some at Corinth had attached undue importance to Paul, Apollos, and Cephas as messengers of the gospel and had created factions in the church. In chapters one and three of the epistle, Paul had lamented their actions and made it clear that he had no desire to be seen as anything other than a servant of God. In chapter four, he pursues this even further by using two additional figures to describe his work as an apostle and evangelist.

First, apostles were "ministers of Christ" (4:1a). The word for "minister" here is different from the one used earlier in the epistle (cf. 1 Cor. 3:5). The Greek word in the former passage is *diakonos*; here it is *hupēretēs*. The words are similar in meaning, and we must not read a radical distinction into them. Both carry the idea of being a servant or assistant to someone else. Robertson and Plummer point out that the latter originally denoted those who pulled the oars on a ship's lower deck. Whether this derivation is in Paul's mind cannot be known. What we are to understand is that he saw himself as one under authority, one taking orders from another.

Second, the apostles were "stewards of the mysteries of God" (4:1b). This is an even more specific definition of th :r role and identifies the nature of the ministry they performed. A "steward" (Gk, *oikonomos*) was a servant entrusted with the routine administration of his master's business. He had authority over other servants, assigned them tasks, and held them responsible for their failures. Yet he was himself always answerable to the master. His position was a responsible one, yet it was not an independent role.

Paul and his fellow-apostles were entrusted with the "mysteries of God" (i.e., the truths of the gospel, 1 Cor. 2:7; cf. Rom. 16:25). Their authority to bind and loose in Jesus' name gave them a position of unique prominence and importance in the church. They remained acutely conscious, however, that their position was a delegated one. The significance of their work lay in the one to whom their message pointed and not in their own persons or deeds.

The apostles and prophets of the first century sought to please God rather than men. They were not vying for personal honor. They realized – as the Corinthians did not – they were nothing of themselves. Whatever responsibility or position their work gave them was due to the grace of God entrusted to them. They had no occasion for personal boasting.

Good "servants" and "stewards" have as their primary goal faithfulness (4:2); they are seeking the approval of their master (4:5). To be judged by the Corinthians or any other human tribunal was immaterial to Paul (4:3a). Even self-judgment was pointless (4:3b-4). Each has his ministry to perform. Let him be about that task – without the desire to be exalted in the eyes of those who witness it or puffed up in his own ego – and leave final judgment about such matters to God alone.

Paul had "transferred" this matter of evaluating men and their ministries to himself and Apollos for the sake of his readers (4:6a). Specifically, he wanted the brethren at Corinth to "learn not to go beyond the things which are written" and not to be "puffed up" in relation to one another (4:6b). As one devotes himself to the study of "the things which are written" (i.e., Holy Scripture), he learns the fundamental truth of subordination. Man is not the measure of all things; to the contrary, man is measured in relation to divine perfection. Understanding this, arrogance and boasting are abandoned. Attaching oneself to men and feeling a sense of pride in that allegiance falls by the way. We have nothing except that which has been given by God – whether natural endowment or assigned ministry (4:7). There is no place for boasting, promoting partisanship within the church, or any similar worldly exercise.

What They Endured For Christ (4:8-21)

As proof of what he had just set forth as a definition of his ministry and that of his associates, Paul reminded the Corinthians of the history of their work. The conduct of their ministries made

it clear they were not seeking to please men but
God.

There is tremendous irony in this section of the
text. Were the saints at Corinth "filled" and "rich"
(4:8), "strong" (4:10), and "puffed up" (4:18-19)? Paul
and his associates in the gospel were "a spectacle
unto the world" (4:9), "fools for Christ's sake" (4:10),
and "made as the filth of the world" (4:13). Why
such a contrast? It was not a matter of actual
standing but *attitude.* The carnal Corinthians were
concerned about status and pride in leaders. Paul
was concerned only that God be glorified. Thus the
apostle begged his readers not to exalt his name
and rally to his honor but to join him in subjecting
all things to Jesus (4:14-16). If only the Corinthians
could show some of the humility which had char-
acterized their teachers!

Paul ends this section of appeal and exhortation
with a warning. Faithful Timothy was coming to
teach among them personally and to call them back
to the rudiments of the faith (4:17). Beyond that,
Paul was planning to come back to Corinth personally (4:18-20; cf. 2 Cor. 2:1ff; 12:14). The tenor of
that visit would be determined by their response
to this epistle: "What will ye? shall I come unto
you with a rod, or in love and a spirit of gentleness?"
(4:21). It would all depend on them.

The "Rights" of Apostles (9:1-23)

From reading the last few lines of chapter four,
one gets the impression that Paul was aware of
some personal opposition to him and his ministry.
Perhaps some of the Apollos-, Cephas-, or Christ-
parties were trying to discredit the Paul-party by
disparaging the man from whom it had named
itself. How typical of controversy that would have
been! Every logician knows about *ad hominem* (i.e.,
against-the-man) arguments in debate. Such "arguments" really do not address the issue at hand

but seek to discredit the person advancing a contrary thesis.

Paul's opponents at Corinth were evidently seeking to discredit him by accusing him of exploiting the church during his initial work in the city. Since we are looking at the nature of the apostolic ministry, it seems proper to move forward to chapter nine for a brief look at Paul's response to this charge. [Note: In its natural setting, chapter nine is part of the apostle's extended argument against insisting on one's "rights" at the expense of another person. We shall not ignore that important thesis in later lessons dealing with some of the internal problems of the church at Corinth. This epistle is so beautifully composed that its pieces interlock at several points.]

In verses 1-14, Paul argues for the *right* that ministers of the Word have to be supported in material things by those they serve. "If we sowed unto you spiritual things, is it a great matter if we shall reap your carnal things?" (9:11; cf. 2 Cor. 11:8; Phil. 4:15-16). In other places Paul taught churches to offer such support: "But let him that is taught in the word communicate unto him that teacheth in all good things" (Gal. 6:6). He could have appealed to the example of Jesus himself, for he allowed people to support him financially during his ministry (Luke 8:1-3).

Verses 15-23 explain why Paul had not asked the people at Corinth to support him in his ministry there, although he did take wages from other churches so he could devote full attention to his ministry there (cf. 2 Cor. 11:7-8). Because of the needs of the Corinthians – and perhaps because of his anticipation of a later charge against himself of the sort some were now making – Paul had foregone that right while with them. "Nevertheless we did not use this right; but we bear all things, that we may cause no hindrance to the gospel of

Christ. ... But I have used none of these things: and I write not these things that it may be so done in my case" (9:12b,15). He would have no one think that his motive for preaching was money.

Paul's concern was the advancement of the gospel and not himself. His preaching was done out of a sense of "necessity" because of his special calling from the Lord; he was looking for a "reward" greater than any which men could give – the reward God gives to those who are faithful at their posts of service in his kingdom (9:16-17; cf. Rev. 2:10). He wanted to be faithful to the "stewardship" he had been given (9:17b; cf. 4:1). "And I do all things for the gospel's sake, that I may be a joint partaker thereof" (9:23).

As to how he actually went about his task, Paul makes the intriguing statement: "For though I was free from all men, I brought myself under bondage to all, that I might gain the more. And to the Jews I became as a Jew ... to them that are under the law, as under the law ... to them that are without law, as without law ... To the weak I became weak, that I might gain the weak: I am become all things to all men, that I may by all means save some" (9:19-22). Here is the reason for Paul's success – and the failure of many of the rest of us – in trying to share the gospel.

Paul started his preaching with an awareness of others and their mindset. He did not isolate himself and declare a hands-off policy toward the world. He took those people seriously in trying to understand where they were in relation to Christ and the gospel. He sought effective means of presentation which would capture their interest – however marginal at the moment – and lead them to faith. He had more than one sermon, one approach.

Have we understood the Christian's obligation to reject the world and its ways as a call to isolation from the people out there who are still enslaved to sin? Jesus went where the sinners were and allowed them to feel comfortable in his presence. Paul tried to put himself in the life situation of those he was approaching to figure out what would strike a spark of interest. This is the right and biblical approach for us to use. Rejecting all false motives for preaching the Word of God (e.g., notoriety, building a following, money), we must work from right motives (e.g., necessity, privilege, compassion) to get the message of Christ before men and women.

A Motivated Ministry (9:24-27)

In his final summary, Paul explains his motive for preaching the gospel at Corinth in the simplest of language. "Do you not know that in a race all the runners run, but only one gets the prize? Run in such a way as to get the prize. Everyone who competes in the games goes into strict training. They do it to get a crown that will not last; but we do it to get a crown that will last forever. Therefore I do not run like a man running aimlessly; I do not fight like a man beating the air. No, I beat my body and make it my slave so that after I have preached to others, I myself will not be disqualified for the prize" (9:24-27 NIV).

When all was said and done, Paul and the other apostles were just like most other Christians. Their single-minded goal was the crown of life. Sacrifice and effort are expended for the sake of receiving it.

Drawing on the imagery of the Isthmian Games, held every three years near Corinth, Paul reminded his readers that contestants in those games were willing to forego certain "rights" to endure the rigors of strict athletic discipline. In the same way, he and the other apostles had foregone certain "rights" they might have claimed for the sake of a much greater goal in their view. For their sakes and his own, Paul was seeking to fulfill his ministry lest he be "disqualified" from his goal.

A Need in Today's Church

The apostles and prophets of the early church are not mythical characters of long ago and far away. They were real persons whose examples and works invite imitation by us.

We have the same gospel those men received and recorded. With the same zeal and devotion they displayed, the result will be the same now as it was centuries ago. The world can be set on its ear!

Paul was once an intense opponent of Christianity but became its most ardent advocate. Many others underwent similar changes. They were *converted* to the Lord Jesus. In their new lives, they worked and endured for Jesus' sake – not to earn their salvation but to show gratitude for the free gift they had received. "But by the grace of God I am what I am: and his grace which was bestowed upon me was not found vain; but I labored more abundantly than they all: yet not I, but the grace of God which was with me" (1 Cor. 15:10). Saved by grace! Serving from gratitude!

Why are we not producing more Pauls today? It appears that we cannot find, train, and equip missionaries for all nations. There seems to be hesitancy in really challenging the secular, unbelieving world with the gospel. The world's mindset and lifestyle are sometimes displayed among people who are members of Christ's church. Toil and sacrifice are words whose meaning are remote from many of us.

Why? *Too many of us are still unconverted.* Yes, it is possible for one to have been baptized, had his name entered on a church roll, and transferred from one congregation to another – without ever having been converted.

Conversion is not "turning over a new leaf." It is something radical. It is like being born anew (John 3:3-5) or dying and rising again (Rom. 6:1-4). It appears that too few of us take it that seriously. The *changes* in thinking, speech, life interests, and behavior which marked those earliest believers are too often lacking in us.

Test yourself against Paul's statement cited earlier from 1 Cor. 15:10. (1) Do you acknowledge the grace of God as the basis of your hope? He saw himself as a sinner without hope, but divine grace reached down and saved him. (2) Do you feel an abiding sense of gratitude for God's grace? Paul did. (3) Do you devote abundant labors to the glory of God out of your thanksgiving? Paul's record is clear.

Maybe some of us just don't feel the deep sense of indebtedness for salvation which Paul felt. Thus we do not have the strong compulsion to service in the kingdom of God he had. Maybe "growing up in the church" is a danger as well as a blessing. Perhaps you have noticed that some of the most active Christians are people who came to the Lord in their mature years! The answer is not to keep people away from Christ until their lives are so mutilated by sin that their salvation is a last-ditch accomplishment which leaves an abiding gratitude for divine grace. That would be a foolish approach, for many would go so far away as to be unreachable. Yet something must be done to avoid leaving the impression that men do God a favor by becoming members of his family.

Conclusion

Speaking to a graduating class at McGill University, the English poet Rudyard Kipling advised the graduates not to care too much for money or power or fame. He said: "Someday you will meet a

man who cares for none of these things – and then
you will know how poor you are."

One has the feeling of having met such a person
when he reads about the apostles and prophets of
the early church. They were not serving in the
flesh, and they were not preoccupied with money
or power or fame. They were serving in the power
of God's Spirit, and their concern was for Christ,
the gospel, and the kingdom of God. They sought
to serve the Lord without shifting the honor from
Jesus to themselves. Their ministry remains the
model for our own.

We cannot do the miraculous works they did. We
can, however, preach the same gospel from the same
pure motives. Troubled churches like the one at
Corinth can be turned around and brought to spiritual health. Lethargic churches can be brought
back to life. The brightest of our young people can
be channeled into ministries for the Lord. The best
of our collective efforts can make a dynamic impact
on a sin-oppressed world.

It must begin in hearts which are grateful for a
redemption purchased by the blood of the Son of
God. Activity can be started by fear and guilt; zeal
and dedication will be maintained only through
gratitude and love.

Study Questions

1. The danger of "allowing healthy appreciation ... to
degenerate into unhealthy adoration" was discussed in
this chapter in connection with Paul, Apollos, and Cephas. Does anything of the same sort happen today? How
can we avoid this pitfall?

2. In referring to the apostles as "ministers of Christ,"
what was Paul's principal point?

3. He also used the term "steward" of himself and his
colleagues. Define the significance of this imagery.

4. How does devotion to "the things which are written"
teach the fundamental truth of subordination to Bible

students? Think of some specific persons, incidents, or passages which teach the lesson dramatically.

5. Verses 8-13 use powerful irony to drive home a point about attitudes people have toward their spiritual status. Reflect on Paul's statements. Try to suggest a modern-day situation comparable to the one he was addressing.

6. How were Paul's opponents at Corinth trying to discredit him? What specific accusation does he deal with at length?

7. Why did Paul forsake his right to ask financial support of the people he taught the gospel in Corinth? In what situations today would an evangelist be wise to make the same decision?

8. Discuss Paul's approach of becoming "all things to all men" for the sake of winning them to Christ. What does this entail? What demands does it make on a person trying to teach the gospel? What methods of teaching should we rethink in light of this methodology in our present work cf evangelism?

9. What was Paul's personal motive for all he did in service to Christ? Is this mere selfishness?

10. Do you agree with the point made in the lesson about the need for "conversion" even among many who have been Christians for a number of years? Explain your answer.

5/ The Leaven of Sin in a Church

1 Cor. 5:1-13

The word *citizenship* refers to a status of full membership in a city, state, or country. The state offers its citizens certain special privileges and agrees to protect them both at home and away. It also expects the loyalty of its people and imposes certain duties on its citizens. An individual who commits treason against his state can lose his citizenship and thereby forfeit all its rights and privileges.

A Christian is one who has a special citizenship. "For our citizenship is in heaven; whence also we wait for a Savior, the Lord Jesus Christ" (Phil. 3:20; cf. Eph. 2:19). Because of this citizenship, he has special privileges and rights of protection within the sphere of divine grace. He also has certain duties to perform. There is also the possibility of forfeiting one's citizenship in the kingdom of heaven and losing all the rights and privileges which go with such a status.

In this study we will see how one can jeopardize

41

his or her heavenly citizenship and forfeit the grace of God. Frightening possibilities will be raised which should warn all believers against laxness in spiritual things. Against the background of a specific problem Paul was forced to deal with among the Corinthians, we shall look at the larger topic of the church's responsibility of self-discipline.

More Distress Over Corinth

The first-century church in the Roman Empire existed as a tiny island of moral purity in a sea of immorality. Fornication, homosexuality, abortion, infanticide, and everything related to these practices were common in Paul's day. When we sometimes lament that our twentieth century is the wickedest of times in history, our lack of historical perspective is betrayed. Among the several times in recorded history which make our own appear ethically conservative, the Roman world of the first century comes to mind quickly.

The sexual chastity preached by apostles and prophets of the early church was practically a novel virtue to the people who heard them. Some observations were made in the opening chapter of this book about the general moral climate at Corinth in particular. There were even religious cults at Corinth which practiced ritual prostitution. It is not difficult to understand how hard it was for people only recently won from such an environment to put their old ways behind them. Thus Paul's correspondence to the Corinthians contains frequent warnings against sexual immorality.

The Shocking Sin (5:1)

Against the background of the apostle's agony over the division within the church at Corinth, he expressed his additional dismay over a case of sexual sin in their midst. The situation involved a man living immorally with his step-mother: "It is actually reported that there is fornication among you, and such fornication as is not even among the Gentiles, that one of you hath his father's wife."

Reading an epistle such as 1 Corinthians is something like listening in on one end of a telephone conversation. Not knowing exactly what has been said on the other end of the line, one lacks details which would make the total conversation more meaningful. Since we don't have the reports from Chloe's household or the letter from Corinth to Paul, we can't reconstruct the case he is dealing with here in precise detail.

We cannot know whether the man's father was dead or not. The woman involved was evidently not a Christian, for the church is given instructions for dealing with the man only. The relationship between the man who was a member of the body of Christ at Corinth and his step-mother was one which Paul found shocking and which would have compromised the whole church. Even in a society so morally lax as Corinth, this sort of incestuous relationship was considered altogether taboo.

The practice of taking close blood relatives and in-laws as marriage partners has been forbidden in all but the earliest days of the human race. The Old Testament prohibited the practice among the Hebrew people (Lev. 18:8; Deut. 22:30). Pagan writers can be cited from the Greeks and Romans who took the same negative view of the practice. The Roman writer Cicero, for example, denounced a marriage between a mother-in-law and son-in-law as "incredible and, apart from this one instance, unheard of" (*Pro Cluentio* 5. 14.).

Reference was made earlier to the first-century church as "an island of moral purity in a sea of immorality." The Corinthian church was no longer such an island in its environment. It had a case of immoral behavior within its ranks which even the pagans would decry.

44

The Church's Attitude (5:2)

As bad as the sin itself, however, was the attitude of the church toward it. While pagans would have been shocked and outraged, the people of God at Corinth were tolerating this gross immorality! "And ye are puffed up, and did not rather mourn, that he that had done this deed might be taken away from among you."

Instead of being shocked and mourning the loss of one of its number to the world, the Corinthians were tolerating his behavior. There is no record which indicates rebuke or censure. Their attitude of being "puffed up" (i.e., arrogant, cf. NIV) over the whole affair indicates nothing of the sort. It may even mean that the man's behavior was defended by some in the church. Against the background of some of Paul's other correspondence, one can imagine that some were arguing that "freedom in Christ" set believers free from conventional moral restraints (Gal. 5:13; cf. 1 Cor. 6:12).

The church is supposed to be patient with its members who are weak and erring, yet penitent. The case at Corinth was not one where a concerned body was gently encouraging a penitent man to come to grips with his moral duties. It was one where a compromised body was improperly defending an impenitent man who was defying fundamental ethical norms.

The Required Action (5:3-8)

Paul was direct and unsparing in his instructions to the church. The impenitent offender was to be "delivered unto Satan" (5:5a). This is simply to say that he was to be denied the rights and privileges of citizenship among the covenant community at Corinth. He was to be barred from the fellowship of the church. Since Satan is the prince of this world (John 12:31; Col. 1:13), excommunicating that erring brother from the church would amount to casting him back into Satan's lap.

The dual purpose behind such an extreme action is stated in these words: "...deliver such a one unto Satan for the destruction of the flesh, that the spirit may be saved in the day of the Lord Jesus" (5:5b).

First, it was hoped the disfellowship would shame the man and awaken him to the enormity of his sin. This, in turn, would move him to put away (i.e., destroy) the works of the flesh which were destined to bar him from heaven (Gal. 5:19-21).

Second, his humility and penitence would allow him to be numbered among the saved at the return of the Lord Jesus.

What Paul was asking the church to do would be painful – both for the man who was the object of the disfellowship and for the body as a whole. Yet the motive was not a vindictive one. The apostle was not asking the church to lash out cruelly against one of its own. He was asking for the entire body to stand together in opposition to the man's evil for the sake of jarring him to his senses and saving him.

There was a real danger to the entire church if this procedure was not followed. By keeping such a person within the ranks of believers, they would be retaining a negative influence which would surely spread and infect others. "Do you not know that a little leaven leavens the whole lump? Cleanse out the old leaven that you may be a new lump, as you really are unleavened" (5:6b-7a).

For the church to shut its eyes to public offenses is not the right or helpful thing to do – either for the individual offender or the church as a whole. Christ has offered himself already as our paschal lamb; we must put away the leaven of sin and walk in sincerity and truth (5:7b-8).

The Church and the World

Christians are to be "lights in the world, holding forth the word of life" (Phil. 2:14-16). This light-bearing function is jeopardized when the high standards of Christian life are not taught and enforced among members of the church in any locality.

Leaving The Planet? (5:9-11)

Paul seems to anticipate an objection to his train of thought at this point. Might someone object that it is not possible to live on planet earth and be separated from sin? Such an objection ignores an obvious limitation. The apostle was talking about the enforcement of discipline among the brethren.

He was not talking about the excommunication of persons "of this world" in giving his counsel – counsel being repeated from his previous letter to Corinth (5:9-10a). After all, Christians and non-Christians were not in a relationship of spiritual fellowship with each other; any consideration of *dis*fellowshipping someone had to point to those already included within their group.

Christians are not obligated to leave the (material) world of planet earth. They are obligated, however, to leave the (spiritual) world which is under the domination of Satan and sin. Among their own number, there must be new norms, new attitudes, and new lives.

Someone within the fellowship who turned back to the old way of life had to know of the body's disapproval. He had to feel their rejection of his sinful and disgraceful behavior. Even social intercourse such as eating with that individual in contexts which implied fraternity had to be broken off (5:11b).

Judging Our Own (5:12-13)

In one sense, the people of God are never to sit in judgment on anyone. We are not to judge by outward appearances (John 7:24). We are not to be capricious and eager to find fault (Matt. 7:1-5). The Lord Jesus Christ is the judge of us all, and we refuse to assume his role (Rom. 14:10).

In another sense, however, there are some judgments which must be made by believers. Leaving final Judgment to the Lord alone, we do respect the doctrines and clearly revealed rules of Christian behavior which he has left for his people. As a matter of internal discipline, flagrant departures from those things must not be tolerated. When an individual is consciously and deliberately following a wicked course, he must be rebuked and brought to repentance. If he persists in sin and will not turn away, there is only one recourse left: "Put away the wicked man from among yourselves" (5:13b). While we have no control over those outside our fellowship, Christ's standards must be respected and enforced within the church.

Church Discipline Today

In an age which glories in its permissiveness and in which few restraints are acknowledged, the Bible remains emphatic in its instruction that discipline is to be practiced among members of the body of Christ. Heaven wants the bride of Christ to be pure and without blemish. Church discipline is the process by which the bride's self-purification is accomplished and she is kept fit for the bridegroom.

When "church discipline" is mentioned, however, several improper conclusions are frequently drawn.

First, some immediately think of withdrawing fellowship from a brother or sister. Excommunication is the last resort of church discipline and is not entertained as a possibility until some other things have been done previously. Only if every reasonable effort to instruct, exhort, and restore a brother has failed does disfellowship enter the picture. Church discipline is a much broader topic than church withdrawal.

Second, church discipline is not a means of "getting even" with someone. It is not to be employed as the tool of personal animosity for preachers and/ or elders to use for the taking of vengeance (cf. Rom. 12:19).

Third, church discipline is not the means of "whipping the brethren in line" on matters of judgment or in areas of honest disagreement about difficult issues. In matters of human opinion and personal preference, the broadest possible latitude should be given each believer (Rom. 14). In matters of doctrine, some subjects are more difficult than others (cf. 2 Pet. 3:16); so long as a teachable and humble spirit before the authority of the Word of God is manifested by all parties concerned and no one attempts to force on another a practice which would violate his conscience, fellowship should be maintained. Even in matters of sinful behavior, we must be patient and kind with an erring Christian (Gal. 6:1); stay close to and give aid to the struggling yet sinful person, and withdraw from only that individual who is deliberately walking in sin (cf. Heb. 10:26).

What, then, is church discipline? Positively, it is the total program of instruction, training, encouragement, and reproof by which the church aids its membership to "grow in the grace and knowledge of our Lord and Savior Jesus Christ" (2 Pet. 3:18) and to "walk in the light as he is in the light" (1 John 1:7). Negatively, it is the exclusion from the church's fellowship of such individuals as are endangering their own souls and/or the souls of others by their high-handed defiance of the will of God (cf. 2 Thess. 3:6).

Sermons, Bible classes, personal encouragement in righteousness – all these are part of the positive aspect of church discipline. Only when these measures fail to have the desired effects of curbing carnal behavior and fostering spiritual growth does one become subject to the church's punitive discipline.

Conclusion

Many persons were committing sins of various sorts at Corinth. In only this one case did Paul specifically call for an action of disfellowship. Why in this one? The answer seems clear: the man was determined and arrogant in his defiance of what was right. Such conduct could not be tolerated among the people of God then, nor can it be countenanced now.

It is something like the discipline of children. A parent can be patient and helpful with a child struggling with any problem – so long as the child is trying to find and do the right thing. When that child turns to deliberate rebellion and attempts to presume on parental love, the line must be drawn. So it is in the church. Love and gentleness are the key words in dealing with wayward saints. The drawing of lines and the severing of fellowship must come, however, when waywardness becomes deliberate and arrogant sin.

Study Questions

1. Why does the subject of sexual immorality come up for discussion so frequently in the Corinthian correspondence?

2. What particular situation of immorality was the church harboring at Corinth? What was the attitude of pagans themselves toward such a relationship?

3. What attitude had the church adopted toward the brother who had committed the sin? What effect would such an attitude have on the man in question?

4. When is a church supposed to be patient and gentle with one of its members who has sinned? When is it expected to be stern?

5. What was the double purpose Paul had in view when he required the excommunication of the sinning brother at Corinth?

6. What was the apostle's fear for the church if this situation was not dealt with quickly and decisively? How reasonable was such a fear?

7. The issue of severing fellowship with a brother raises the question of the positive nature of fellowship. What does the term signify? If one is excommunicated, what relationships may Christians continue with him?

8. In what circumstances are Christian forbidden to judge others? Under what conditions are Christians required to make judgments about others?

9. Discuss the mistaken ideas of church discipline which circulate so freely among Christians. Are there other false notions you can add to the list given in the book?

10. Give your own definition of *church discipline*. Be sure to include both a positive and negative aspect in your definition.

6/ Transformed People And Their Obligations

1 Cor. 6:1-20

An expedition of scientists set out to capture a certain species of monkey that lived in the jungles of Africa. Because they wanted to bring the animals back unharmed, they studied their habits carefully to devise a strategy for their capture. The trap they used turned out to be very simple, but totally efficient.

They took jars with long, slender necks. Nuts were put in the jars as bait. The monkeys came to the jars, thrust in their paws, and grasped the nuts. With their paws clinched, they could not get free of the heavy jars! Unwilling to let go of the nuts because of their possessive natures, the monkeys, screaming in fear, were held until their captors arrived to take them away.

We smile at the foolishness of the monkeys. Don't we often fall into the same trap? Don't we "make monkeys of ourselves" by refusing to let go certain things that have us caught in a trap?

The Bible occasionally gives lists of some things people must let go in order to be new creatures – things such as lying, anger, stealing, bitterness, and the like (cf. Col. 3:5-10). These things are traps to the human spirit. We can be free only by letting them go.

Then the old things have to be replaced with a new way of life. Instead of lying, speak the truth to people. Instead of stealing, do productive work and share what you earn with others. Instead of bitterness, learn to be forgiving and patient with the people around you (cf. Eph. 4:29-32).

Christians are supposed to be different. Our profession of faith in Jesus obligates us to imitate him. Conversion is supposed to mark a point of radical new changes in one's behavior.

In his correspondence with the troubled and carnal Corinthians, Paul labored to show them the moral and spiritual implications of their relationship to Jesus Christ. He wanted them to catch a vision of the type of life they should be living as God's people. In chapter six, he pointed to two serious instances of their failure to keep worldly ways out of the church. First, there was the matter of litigation before unbelievers. Second, there was the challenge of sexual impurity in the wicked environment of Corinth. So typical of unbelievers to quarrel and give way to carnal lusts. Unthinkable for men and women wearing the name of Christ!

Get Along With One Another

A most obvious difference the world should observe in Christians is a spirit of love and peace within their fellowship. If people still in the world are competitive, jealous, and hateful with one another, those persons who have been called out of the world by the gospel should put such things away. Christians are sons and daughters of the Living God. This means they are brothers and sisters within a great spiritual family.

While eating the Passover meal with the apostles on the evening of his betrayal, Jesus said: "By this shall all men know that ye are my disciples, if ye have love one to another" (John 13:35). Around the beginning of the third century, Tertullian could write: "But it is mainly the deeds of a love so noble that lead many to put a brand on us. 'See,' they say, 'how they love one another,' for they themselves are animated by mutual hatred; 'see how they are ready even to die for one another,' for they themselves will rather put to death" (*Apology* 39).

The people at Corinth were having trouble getting along with one another. Their love for one another was not evident. There was strife, rancor, and litigation. The problem had to be addressed by the apostle.

Litigation Among Saints (6:1-6)

In the first-century world, Greeks were fond of using the law courts. On the flimsiest of pretexts, one would bring a charge against his neighbor and attempt to bring easy financial gain to himself. The situation was much like our own is coming to be, when public officials, doctors, and large corporations are "sued for damages" on the flimsiest of pretexts by greedy and dishonest persons.

Paul was attempting to discourage Christian participation in such nonsensical lawsuits. His method was to attempt to shame his readers in the pagan city of Corinth: "Dare any of you, having a matter against his neighbor, go to law before the unrighteous, and not before the saints? ...I say this to move you to shame. What, cannot there be found among you one wise man who shall be able to decide between his brethren, but brother goeth to law with brother, and that before unbelievers" (6:1,5-6).

A Forgotten Principle (6:7-8)

In such trivial matters, one should "take wrong" and "be defrauded" (6:7b). Or, to use the words of the Lord, he should "turn the other cheek" (cf. Mt.5:38-39).

It would be a gross oversimplification, however, to assume that the counsel of the apostle to the Corinthians bars recourse to courts by Christians under all circumstances.

For one thing, such an interpretation contradicts other passages of Scripture. The Lord taught that one whose partner has committed fornication can divorce that person and remarry (Matt. 19:9). If John and Mary are members of the church and John is unfaithful to Mary, she has the right to "go to law" with a brother to sue for dissolution of the marriage. If Paul's teaching here is without qualification, no Christian could ever divorce a Christian companion who has violated the sanctity of marriage.

Second, understanding this text as an absolute prohibition of going into the courts with a brother leads to absurdities. Suppose a member of the church became reprobate to the faith and began suing Christians for various amounts of money; suppose he even sued the entire church for possession of its property. According to one view of 1 Cor. 6, faithful believers could not counter his suits and defend themselves and their property.

Third, elders and other brethren who might hear disputes between saints have no right to handle some issues. Can a group of elders grant someone a divorce? Can a business meeting force the repayment of a loan or handle a foreclosure? The idea is absurd. These are responsibilities which God has granted to the civil government, and civil government is a "minister of God to thee for good" (Rom.13:4) in fulfilling its obligations.

In summary, then, here is Paul's inspired teaching about members of the church and civil law courts. (1) Christians should not take offense with one another in the everyday affairs of life. (2) If some offense does arise which cannot be settled between the two brothers involved, let them seek the counsel and mediation of faithful brethren. This allows the issue to be resolved without having the church embarrassed by the spectacle of its members being litigious with one another before unbelievers. (3) If the matter cannot be settled to the full satisfaction of both parties, the aggrieved person should turn the other cheek and suffer wrong before resorting to the courts. (4) In matters of such significance that the church has neither the right nor resources to try to resolve them (i.e., in matters greater than mere personal offense), God has ordained civil governments to establish a system of courts for their resolution. (5) Christians do not sin when they use the courts for their legitimate purposes.

Keep Yourselves Pure

Another obligation of the new life in Christ is moral uprightness. Christians are called to walk in sanctification and purity.

Given the moral climate of Corinth, it would have been an easy thing for the church there to be infected with worldly attitudes and behavior. Thus warnings and encouragements about ethics – especially sexual ethics – are given throughout the epistle.

Cleansed By Christ (6:9-11)

There is no observable difference between the world and the church unless righteousness is found among the people of God. If Christians quarrel in the courts just as their non-Christian neighbors do, what is the difference between them? If Christians are thieves and drunkards just as their non-Christian neighbors are, how can they be "salt" and "light" to the world? If Christians are homosexuals and fornicators just as their non-Christian neighbors are, how can they speak of purity and be taken seriously?

"Or know ye not that the unrighteous shall not inherit the kingdom of God? Be not deceived: neither fornicators, nor idolaters, nor adulterers, nor effeminate, nor abusers of themselves with men, nor thieves, nor covetous, nor drunkards, nor revilers, nor extortioners, shall inherit the kingdom of God" (6:9-10). The point of these two verses is clear enough: living an unrighteous life disqualifies one from the kingdom of God.

The people at Corinth had repudiated the sins of immorality Paul named at the time of their baptism. "And such were some of you: but ye were washed, but ye were sanctified, but ye were justified in the name of the Lord Jesus Christ, and in the Spirit of our God" (6:11).

Why would they go back to a way of life which had been renounced earlier? Perhaps a clue is found in the next three verses. Some at Corinth may have been arguing that Christian "freedom" allowed them to do as their pleased with their lives.

Immorality Not Permitted (6:12-14)

The slogan of some of the Corinthians must have been "Everything is lawful!" (cf. RSV, NIV). They were like certain brethren among the churches of Galatia who wanted to interpret Christian freedom as license. Paul wrote: "You, my brothers, were called to be free. But do not use your freedom to indulge your sinful nature" (Gal. 5:13 NIV).

The "freedom-lovers" were saying that sexual desire is the same as desire for food. Both are natural; both deserve to be satisfied. Whenever either urge is felt, one should move to satisfy it!

Paul recoiled from such a notion in holy horror. For one thing, there are limits on what Christians should do in areas of life where "lawful" rights are under consideration. The two parameters identified here are these: (1) some things are not "expedient" (i.e., helpful) to believers in their new lives and (2) some are capable of enslaving Christians to their passions. Take eating and drinking as an illustration. Paul will later argue in chapter ten that even so common a freedom as that to eat and drink is limited by these considerations. Everything must be done with the glory of God in view (1 Cor. 10:31).

At an even deeper level, however, Paul responds to the libertines at Corinth by challenging their notion that the appetite for sex is as innocuous as that for food. "Meats for the belly, and the belly for meats: but God shall bring to nought both it and them. But the body is not for fornication, but for the Lord; and the Lord for the body: and God both raised the Lord, and will raise up us through his power" (6:13-14).

Yes, the stomach was created to crave food and use it for the maintenance of the biological organism. Oneday both the stomach and the foods it craves will perish. The same is not true, however, of the human body as a totality. Stomach, liver, kidneys, and corneas are incidental and transient parts of a greater whole. A human being is greater than the sum of his or her parts, for he or she is an ensouled body in God's own image.

Furthermore, as a totality, an embodied human is capable of personal relationships – with both God and other human beings. Food taken into the stomach does not defile one's personhood (cf. Matt. 15:11), but wrong relationships do. To use one's body to enter a God-forbidden relationship (e.g., fornication) is to violate one's personality and likeness to God.

58

Some things are forbidden to people set free in
Christ. All the works of the flesh are off limits, for
they will keep one from the kingdom of God (cf.
Gal. 5:19-21). To appeal to "freedom" and "grace"
in justification of such deeds is monstrously evil.

Members Of Christ (6:15-18)

Another powerful reason for abstaining from
immorality is found in the Christian's relationship
to Christ's spiritual body. All saved persons are
"members of Christ" (6:15a). By being baptized
into him, both body and spirit of the convert were
joined to Christ. Taking that same person and join-
ing him or her with a prostitute is therefore an
unthinkable act. "Shall I then take away the members of Christ, and make them members of a harlot?
God forbid" (6:15b). The unions are mutually exclu-
sive. To be intimately connected with Christ pre-
cludes unions with harlots; to have sexual relations
with prostitutes violates one's union with Christ.
For this reason, Christians must "flee fornication"
(6:18a).

At this point in his discussion, Paul makes a
most interesting observation about sexual sin:
"Every sin that a man doeth is without the body;
but he that committeth fornication sinneth against
his own body" (6:18b). What does he mean?

The reasoning here builds on the facts already
established in the chapter about personhood and
union with Christ. Since we are not animals but
human beings in the image of God, sex is not merely
"mating"; it is the union of bodies and spirits, the
linking of two total personalities. Since we are
members of Christ's spiritual body, sex is not altogether private to two people; Christ himself is a
participant in every event in that person's life.
Stealing someone else's belongings is different from
fornication for these reasons. Stealing does not involve and deny personhood in the way fornication

does. The former is external to one's bodily being and may be done impersonally and anonymously; the latter involves the body and personality in its very nature.

Temples Of The Spirit (6:19-20)

Finally, Paul reminds his readers that Christians are not only attached to Christ's spiritual body but are also indwelt by the Holy Spirit. The glory of God dwells with Christians through the presence of the Spirit. The body of each believer is a "temple" of the Spirit.

If fornication is antithetical to the fact of one's union with Christ, it is certainly defiling to the temple which God's Spirit inhabits. The sin is uniquely wrong and cannot be justified among the people of God. Bought with so great a price as the blood of the Son of God, Christians belong to God and must seek ways to glorify him through the body.

The doctrine of the indwelling Spirit is filled with comfort. We know we are not alone in our struggles with sin. He is present to strengthen us against sin and to provide stamina for daily battles against evil (cf. Eph. 3:14-16). The doctrine is also filled with great challenge. The challenge is to live with the consciousness of his presence and to keep oneself undefiled as his temple.

Conclusion

Transformed people have the obligation of keeping the spirit and behavior of the world outside the church.

In a world of hate, the church must be an example of a loving fellowship. Following Christ's command, believers must let men know they are his through our love for one another. The family of God must live as a family – tolerantly, flexibly, patiently. There must be no fighting within the group which embarrasses Christ before unbelievers. Lawcourts and other public exchanges of charge and countercharge must be avoided. Otherwise the church is a spectacle before the world. Love for one another as brothers and sisters will overcome this human tendency toward rivalry and exploitation of others.

In a world of vice and immorality, the church must be an island of moral uprightness. While being concerned about that world and attempting to evangelize it, we cannot be immersed in its culture. We cannot adopt its lifestyle and seek to justify concessions to the flesh. Greed, idolatry, and drunkenness surround the church; they must not be allowed within the church. In particular, sexual sins – because of their implications against both deity and human personality – must be resisted with diligence.

Unlike foolish monkeys or brutish men, the people of God refuse to be trapped by the vices of the past. They have let them go in order to be free of their hold.

Study Questions

1. What are some of the "traps" of the human spirit which must be let go for Christ's sake? What are the positive virtues with which those evils are to be replaced?

2. Discuss John 13:35 in some detail. In what context did Jesus speak these words? What was their immediate relevance to that setting? What is their abiding significance to us?

3. How were civil courts commonly used in Paul's day? What modern parallels do you see to this?

4. Under what circumstances should Christians "take wrong" and "be defrauded"? In what context are believers justified in going into court?

5. Go over the five summary points given in this chapter about Paul's teaching on a Christian's use of civil

courts. Do you agree with these points? Which would you modify? What would you add?

6. The topic of "freedom" seems to have been terribly important at Corinth. How was this word being used to justify immorality?

7. What was Paul's reaction to the position of the "freedom-lovers"?

8. Discuss the apostle's discussion of personhood and human relationships in relation to the matter of fornication.

9. How does the topic of the indwelling of the Spirit of God relate to sexual purity?

10. This chapter speaks of the *comfort* and *challenge* of the doctrine of doctrine of the indwelling Holy Spirit. Explain each.

7/ Counsel About Marriage

1 Cor. 7:1-40

A radiant bride and a nervous groom stand before a minister and solemnly repeat their marriage vows. He pronounces them husband and wife. They kiss, the camera fades away, and they live happily ever after. So goes the celluloid representation of marriage of a generation ago. It was unrealistic then and almost forgotten now.

Today's young people see a different version of human relationships on the silver screen. They see – in graphic detail – sex without love or commitment. They see couples grabbing satisfaction for the moment without any thought for tomorrow. Trained by Hollywood, each generation harbors its false illusions.

Who has a clearer view? Neither sees it as it really is. The Bible view of love and marriage stands in sharp juxtaposition to both.

Yesterday's bride, faced with the reality of dishes and diapers, soon discovered that she had been misled. The marriage had occasional thorns along with the roses she had expected. The hopeful groom also had his awakening. As real life crowded out fantasy, some of those couples adjusted and made good marriages. But many failed to do so. The divorce rate testifies to the number who said "I do" and then didn't.

Today's couple is also learning that the movie script for life and love has been a sham. A few unhappy experiences and several morning-after episodes of loneliness and guilt have taught them that sex without love is empty. Today doesn't have to look to tomorrow, but tomorrow will always have to look back to today.

A Biblical Perspective

God made it clear from the beginning that it was not good for man to be alone. He made a woman to be his companion and helper. He brought the two together and instructed them to hold fast to one another in loving commitment (Gen. 2:18-25). The Bible says: "He who finds a wife finds a good thing, and obtains favor from the Lord" (Prov. 18:22).

As we will see from 1 Cor. 7, there is no obligation that anyone has to get married and have a family. In fact, Paul himself was unmarried. He even recommended the single life to certain people and for certain circumstances.

Times have changed drastically from Paul's day to ours. Marriage as an institution will probably never again be what it once was. Social barriers have crumbled and women have gained more economic independence from men. The traditional marriage in which the man goes to work and the woman stays home to take care of babies is giving way to dual-career marriages. People wait longer to marry and expect more of the relationship than their parents did. We can't turn back the clock and make society what it was fifty or a hundred years ago – much less what it was in the first century. What we can do, however, is keep reminding people that some things about the nature of marriage do not change with the passing of time or shifts in societal living patterns.

The biblical view of marriage is more than that of two people who just happen to live under the same roof. They are sharing a life – with all its joys and sorrows. When they become "one flesh," it is more than a sexual union. It is an acknowledgment of their interdependence. Jesus reminded us that "from the beginning" God made the human race "male and female" (Matt. 19:4). When one male and one female enter a marriage commitment, they cannot be independent of one another. They must share a common life under Christ. As Paul once wrote to husbands and wives: "Be subject to one another out of reverence for Christ" (Eph. 5:21).

Questions From Corinth

With all the problems created for the church at Corinth by its immoral environment, one would have been surprised not to find some involving marriage. The generally low moral standards of that wicked city must have made it hard for anyone to hold this sacred relationship in the esteem it deserves.

First Corinthians is a carefully structured epistle. In the first six chapters, the apostle treats a number of issues (especially division in the church) which he had evidently learned about through Chloe's household (cf. 1 Cor. 1:11). Then, in chapters 7-16, he responds to several questions which had been put to him in written form from the brethren of that city (cf. 7:1a). Perhaps the letter containing the questions had been delivered to him by the delegation mentioned in the final chapter of the epistle (1 Cor. 16:17).

In each case with the written questions, he appears to preface his responses with the formula "now concerning." If this is correct, the questions were about marriage (7:1-40), things sacrificed to idols (8:1 – 11:1), worship (11:2-34), gifts of the Holy Spirit (12:1 – 14:40), the resurrection (15:1-58), and the collection for poor saints in Judea (16:1-4).

Paul's Counsel on Marriage

The first issue addressed in the second section of the epistle is marriage. The topic was evidently as vital and urgent for first-century Christians as it is for us. That Paul dealt with it at such length and touched on so many related topics (e.g., celibacy, widows, etc.) indicates he shared that view.

Marriage And Celibacy (7:1-9)

Corinth was such an immoral city that some Christians there must have been urging the single life as the only safe option open to God's people in such an environment. Or perhaps the ascetic teachings of some group within the church had come to have influence there. At any rate, the issue of celibacy looms large as background for the entire chapter.

Some have understood Paul to disparage the married state in these verses. Such a view has to read something into the text which is certainly not apparent on the surface and sets the apostle against what he said himself in Ephesians 5:22ff.

There is certainly nothing wrong with celibacy. To be sure, Paul points out that he had chosen that life for himself (7:7a) and will later indicate some of its advantages (7:32-35). Throughout the chapter, however, he assumes marriage to be the norm and makes it clear that his purpose is not to dissuade people from getting married (7:7b, 9, 28). From the use made of the expression "it is good" in the chapter (cf. 7:1, 8, 26), it appears that Paul is giving a *practical* (as opposed to moral) judgment about the advisability of foregoing marriage under the peculiar circumstance of trial which believers were facing at Corinth when he wrote this letter (7:26).

Over against his practical judgment about the advantages of the single life was a *moral consideration* which was more crucial. "But, because of fornications, let each man have his own wife, and let each woman have her own husband" (7:2). In a large city such as Corinth, where sexual sin was commonplace, the temptations facing an unmarried adult must have been tremendous. So, in spite of whatever practical advantages Paul may have pointed to, marriage remained the norm for most believers. Robertson and Plummer have noted:

> This passage is sometimes criticized as a very low view of marriage. But the apostle is not discussing the characteristics of the ideal married life; he is answering questions put to him by Christians who had to live in such a city as Corinth. In a society so full of temptations, he advises marriage, not as the lesser of two evils, but as a necessary safeguard against evil. So far from marriage being wrong, as some Corinthians were thinking, it was for very many people a duty.

Having granted the married state to be the norm, Paul writes of the habitual attention to each other's sexual needs which a husband and wife must recognize and meet. The champions of asceticism at Corinth must have held a view like this: if not celibate, then at least self-denying in sexual life. Such a view is wrong, for it ignores the fact that one owes something to his or her partner in marriage. The man who thought himself spiritual at Corinth by foregoing normal sexual contact with his wife was sinning against her (7:3-4). It is a form of "fraud" when one denies his or her partner these intimacies (7:5a). Abstention can be allowed only when it is (1) by mutual consent, (2) for some good purpose, and (3) for a temporary period (7:5b).

After all, these were only practical judgments and not divine commands concerning celibacy (7:6). No one can tell another what he must do in the matter (7:7). Again, he reminded his readers, moral considerations always have precedence over practical ones; one should marry rather than "burn with passion" (NIV) and be tempted to commit fornication (7:8-9).

Divorce (7:10-16)

Turning next to those saints at Corinth who were married, Paul gives the counsel one would expect to hear from a Christian: make your marriages work, and do not even consider divorce as a genuine option. "But unto the married I give charge, yea not I, but the Lord, That the wife depart not from her husband (but should she depart, let her remain unmarried, or else be reconciled to her husband); and that the husband leave not his wife" (7:10-11).

Believers are supposed to live out their marital commitments in love and fidelity. Marriage between two Christians should be such as to demonstrate in a most practical way to non-Christians the sanctifying power of Christ's presence in their lives. In saying that this charge was not his own but the Lord's (i.e., "yea not I, but the Lord"), Paul appears to be saying that he was simply quoting the words of Jesus on the matter at hand (cf. Luke 16:18).

But what if a marriage just doesn't work? What if two people simply "make a mistake" in marriage? Ancient Corinthians and modern Americans would tend to answer, "Get a divorce and try again with someone else." That is not a biblical answer. Inspired counsel to such a couple allows them to admit defeat in their marriage and to "de-part" (i.e., end their marriage). It does not give them the right to marry again. Their options are limited to two: (1) remain unmarried or (2) work out their problems and be reconciled. Here, then, is a situation where divorce might occur and the people involved still both be saved. [Note: Our "legal separation" was unknown in antiquity and this text clearly envisions the prospect of divorce. The word *chorizō* means "to separate, to divide" and is used in the papyri as a technical expression for divorce. Cf. Matt. 19:6.] We need to remember this option for troubled couples today. It is our tendency to assume that at least one – if not both – of the parties to any failed marriage will be lost to Christ and his church.

In verses 12-16, the special situation of a Christian married to an unbeliever (i.e., "the rest") is considered. When Paul wrote that his counsel to these people was his own rather than Christ's (i.e., "say I, not the Lord"), he should not be misunderstood. He was not disclaiming authority for his teaching. To the contrary, he would later say that all his teaching had divine authority behind it (7:40b; 14:37). On the assumption that Jesus' teaching had first application to his own disciples, what relevance did his view of divorce have to a mixed marriage? Paul's authority as an apostle allowed him to answer.

The will of God for a mixed marriage is the same as it is for one where both are Christians. The marriage is to be kept together and made to work. "And the woman that hath an unbelieving husband, and he is content to dwell with her, let her not leave her husband" (7:13). The reason? Her husband and children are "sanctified" and made "holy" by her presence in that family. Both English words are from the same Greek root which means "set apart, consecrated." It is not that the non-

Christian husband and children are saved through the believer's presence. It is rather that the believer's presence is God's means of laying claim to them. Through the Christian, it is God's intention to call the husband and children unto himself in faith (cf. 1 Pet. 3:1-2).

"Yet if the unbelieving departeth, let him depart: the brother or sister is not under bondage in such cases: but God has called us in peace" (7:15). Divorce from an unbeliever was not to be initiated by the Christian. But if the unbeliever initiated it, the believer need not feel bound in trying to keep the marriage alive. The Christian has no servile obligation (Gr, *ou dedoulōtai* = has not been enslaved) to the unbeliever and is not to subject herself to pointless humiliation. Even wanting to keep the marriage together for the sake of converting the other family members has its limitations. It will not always happen that way (7:16). As with the situation envisioned earlier in the chapter (cf. 7:10-11), there are two options open to the divorced parties which will not compound their lives with the sin of adultery: (1) remain unmarried or (2) be reconciled. No third option of seeking another companion is offered to either party.

Living A Christian Calling (7:17-24)

Having called for Christians to live in peace (7:15b), Paul explores that theme for a few lines and makes some practical applications of it. "Only, as the Lord hath distributed to each man, as God hath called each, so let him walk. And so ordain I in all the churches" (7:17).

God's people must live so as to glorify their Savior in whatever circumstance they are in. Of course, one cannot glorify God in sin. Thus if one were called in drunkenness, fornication, or idolatry, he certainly could not remain in those conditions. There is no glory for God in such circumstances – except as he brings people out of them.

Yet God can be glorified in other situations which entail difficulties. Is it harder to follow Christ while married to an unbeliever? Certainly so. Yet, since that situation is not itself sinful, one must remain with the marriage – so long as the unbeliever is willing – and glorify God in it. Some are Jews and others are Gentiles (7:18-20); some are slaves and others are free (7:21-23). These ethnic and social considerations sometimes seem all-important to us. In the sight of God, they matter for nothing. We are all one in Christ Jesus (Gal. 3:28) and should view all things of this world and its order as insignificant when compared with eternal realities.

Paul is not approving slavery as an institution here any more than he is approving abuses which occur within some marriages. He is simply dealing with practical realities and assuring believers that God will give strength to surmount the challenges they face in any situation. Whining brings no victories and resentment gives God no glory. Whether Greek or Jew, slave or free, married to a believer or unbeliever – these conditions do not alter one's relationship to Christ or jeopardize his spiritual security.

Marriage In A Context Of Stress (7:25-38)

About virgins and their plans concerning marriage, Paul begins his counsel with a disclaimer similar to the one in verse 12. There is no "commandment" from Jesus as to whether one must marry by a certain age or at all. Yet, as one made trustworthy by the Spirit's guidance (cf. 7:40b), Paul proceeds to give his apostolic "judgment" on the matter.

Verse 26 is the key to this section. There was some sort of "distress" pressing the saints at Corinth. Under that peculiar circumstance, it was best for people to remain as they were. That is, one should not complicate an already complex situation by adding the special challenge of beginning married life at Corinth in the mid-first century.

We must simply admit that we do not know what the "distress" was. The most likely explanation is that Paul foresaw persecutions for the believers at Corinth – if and when they began to take their spiritual commitments more seriously (cf. 1 Pet. 4:3-4). On the assumption that his letter would have the desired effect among them, he did not want them to add to their problems the natural preoccupation and distractions that would come to one who was altering his basic lifestyle as to family relationships. "But I would have you to be free from cares. He that is unmarried is careful for the things of the Lord, how he may please the Lord: but he that is married is careful for the things of the world, how me may please his wife, and is divided" (7:32-34a).

Paul assumed that anyone getting married would give great amounts of time and attention to the new partner and the structuring of a good relationship with him or her. This reflects his upbringing in Judaism (cf. Deut. 24:5) and stands in contrast with today's carelessness in nurturing new marriages. (For that matter, ending a marriage – even under the circumstances envisioned in verses 11 or 15 – would also be most unwise because of the problems that would generate. Cf. 7:27a.)

The apostle's own life was a good example in this regard. Under the situation of stress he accepted as a missionary, he had chosen to forego marriage (1 Cor. 9:5). Concern for his own safety and health were often set aside for the sake of a perilous mission. It would have been very different to disregard those same factors if a wife and children had been involved. One can make personal sacrifices which he has no right to unilaterally impose on others under his authority.

Even so, Paul admitted that there was no sin

involved in marrying under those circumstances (7:28a). He was merely counseling caution for the sake of sparing unnecessary hardships to his readers (7:28b). "I say this for your own benefit, not to lay any restraint upon you, but to promote good order and to secure your undivided devotion to the Lord" (7:35 RSV).

Another problem in this section of the chapter is not only uncertainty over the nature of the problem situation being faced at Corinth when Paul wrote but legitimate disagreement over the person being addressed in verses 36-38. The King James and American Standard Versions indicate the issue to be the attitude of fathers toward their unmarried daughters; the Revised Standard and New International Versions tend to the view that it is the behavior of a man toward his betrothed which is intended. Good arguments can be made in favor of either interpretation. Because of verse 37, the latter position may seem to be preferable. As Barrett observes, it is "very difficult to apply this advice to the case of a father with his unmarried daughter"; the picture, however, of a "young man who is able to master his natural desire to marry his fiancee is perfectly clear."

Remarriage Among Widows (7:39-40)

The final question Paul addresses concerning marriage is this: May widows remarry?

Against the Christian understanding that marriage is for life, some were evidently wondering if the relationship extended even into the world beyond. If it does, obvious problems would be created. If a woman's husband died and she remarried, whose wife would she be in the resurrection? This same question was once put to Jesus (Matt. 22:23-33). Others at Corinth, knowing the Jewish law about levirate marriage, may have wondered if a widow was restricted in a second marriage to the brother of the companion who had died.

Paul's answer was direct and clear. Marriage is terminated by the death of either companion. In such a case, the surviving partner is "free to be married to whom she wishes, only in the Lord" (7:39). Some have taken "only in the Lord" to mean that the second partner must be a Christian. That would be a severe restriction of Paul's meaning, for he is not discussing the person the widow marries but the manner of forming her new union. This is to say that the restriction is to the effect that her new marriage must honor Christ's laws on the subject and must not be one that would interfere with her duties as a Christian. A similar use and meaning for "in the Lord" occurs at Ephesians 6:1; children are to obey not just Christian parents but whatever instructions they receive from their mothers and fathers which are compatible with the will of Christ.

Again Paul gives his advice that an unmarried person -- in this case a widow -- is better advised at Corinth to remain single under the present distress (7:40).

Conclusion

Just as at Corinth in the first century, marriage remains the norm for most people today. More than 90 percent of the population will eventually marry. Even the vast majority of those who go through the trauma of divorce will try again to experience wedded bliss. And just as at Corinth, there are still a great many questions which can be raised as to the doctrinal and practical implications of this most intimate of all human relationships. How we might wish an inspired apostle were still around to be consulted on them!

Good marriages are not the result of "fate" or "good luck." They are not the fruit of finding one's "one and only love" in the world. They are created when a man and a woman are consciously surrendered to the way of life described in the Word of God. There is no greater blessing which can come to one in this life than to be a partner to such a union.

Study Questions

1. Comment on and expand the discussion in this chapter about "false illusions" of marriage which have been fostered through various media over the years. What false illusions have we fostered in Sunday School and pulpit?

2. Explain the structural features of this epistle to Corinth. How certain can we be about the precise formulation of the questions put to Paul?

3. Some commentators insist that Paul displays a negative attitude toward marriage. Do you agree? Defend your answer.

4. Some at Corinth were apparently encouraging sexual self-denial among married Christians. What was Paul's response? How might one be guilty of "fraud" in marriage?

5. If a marriage ends in divorce yet without infidelity on the part of either person, what options do the parties have? Must we assume that at least one person in every situation of divorce will be lost to Christ and the church? How can we minister to such individuals?

6. What special responsibilities are there for persons married to non-Christians? In what sense does the believer "sanctify" the unbeliever and their children?

7. Discuss the difficulties Paul referred to which come to people in situations of special challenge (7:17-24). How do these situations become opportunities to Christians?

8. Paul urged saints to be cautious about entering marriage under situations of stress. Can you think of some modern contexts where couples would be better advised to wait about marriage?

9. What was the apostle's counsel concerning the remarriage of widows?

10. What is the meaning of the expressions "yea not I, but the Lord" (7:10) and "say I, not the Lord" (7:12) in this chapter? Are there uninspired sections in this epistle?

8/ Freedom: Its Reality and Limits

1 Cor. 8:1 –11:1

In the list of questions put to Paul from the church at Corinth, the second one had to do with Christians eating meat which had been offered to idols. To answer the question, Paul went into an extended discussion of *personal freedom* among believers.

Paul tied two themes together in his discussion: knowledge and love. On the basis of *knowledge,* one could be assured of certain freedoms he has the right to exercise. For the sake of *love,* however, he might choose to forego some of them.

The issue at stake here is much larger than one might think at first. It has many practical implications for our own time and for our behavior in relation to both the church and the world. Few of us will ever make a decision about eating meat which has been used as a sacrifice to an idol. All of us will face issues related to the use of our Christian liberty.

Insofar as the conscience and spiritual life of a

believer are concerned, there may be things he or she can do without the slightest compunction. Out of deference to someone else, however, he or she may forego that thing rather than become a stumbling block to another believer or a hindrance to someone outside the body of Christ.

Paul's approach to the problem is to establish the principle of love for one's fellow believers as the primary factor in dealing with this issue in chapter eight, use his own situation as an apostle as an illustration of one who chooses to forego certain rights in chapter nine, and finally appeal to the example of the ancient Israelites as people who fell into idolatry because of their foolish toying with it in chapter ten.

Background Information

It would be much easier to interpret Paul on these issues if we had fuller knowledge of the situation to which he was speaking. We have to piece together two or three bits of information from our text to understand what was at stake. If we fail to see the different shades of the problem, we will become terribly confused with the solution the apostle offered.

Today it seems rather straightforward and simple to us that Christians can have no participation in idol worship. Once a person is converted from a false religion, he must walk away from its trappings and involve himself in the things of his new faith. Such a view of the matter may suffice for our time, but the situation in Corinth was much more complex.

Practically all social life in a city like Corinth involved contact with idolatry. Almost every city had a patron deity who was honored at all public events. Whereas we sing the national anthem before major sporting events, the people of Corinth would have offered sacrifices to the appropriate deities and sponsored a communal meal. What should a Christian do? Was it his duty to become a social recluse and to abstain from civic life?

It would be easy enough to stay away from the pagan temples and worship rites on holy days, but there were things like weddings and funerals. Such events would take place in idol temples and would surely involve taking a meal there. The food would consist of meat sacrificed to the idol, and the entire meal would be consecrated to Apollo, Isis, Aphrodite, or some other false god.

Added to these public situations where Christians would be under pressure to compromise themselves with idolatry were numerous private ones. One still had non-Christian family and friends. There might be a professional guild in which one held membership and whose wrath he could ill afford in his business. At all such gatherings it would be most likely that a sacrifice would be offered in connection with any meals to be shared. The meat served would likely have been used in a pagan ceremony or worship context.

Finally, there was the possibility that meats purchased in the local butcher shops were somehow tainted through association with idols. The larger portion of most sacrifices went to the priests. Any that he and his family did not need for personal use might be taken to the market and sold as surplus to the meat merchants. Then when served at a neighbor's house or when eating from one's own table, there was always the possibility that what was eaten had been used previously as a sacrifice to an idol. Was the meat defiled? Would its association with a pagan deity somehow harm a Christian spiritually?

Perhaps you are ready with answers to all the situations posed above. But remember that you are dealing with the subject with the advantage of a hindsight those people did not have. They were first-generation Christians trying to settle all these things in their minds. It was no small task, and they wrote to Paul for guidance.

Examining the Text

There appear to have been three positions and three groups of Corinthian Christians on this matter: the conceited, the conscientious, and the confused. The *conceited* brethren had adopted a posture of superior wisdom. Affirming that idols were nothing, they not only ate meat from the shops but went to public events and participated in the idol feasts. The *conscientious* brethren refused to take part in the public festivals which honored false gods; they wanted no part in the worship of Zeus or Athena. They even were scrupulous about the meat they ate from a neighbor's table and would question its possible connection with an idol. They would inquire of the butcher about the exact origin of the meat they were about to buy. Between these two extreme positions were the *confused* Christians who did not know what to do.

Paul's answer to their questions was both high in tone and practical of application.

Eating Meat Offered To Idols (8:1-13)

The first few lines are addressed to the conceited ones. Were they insisting "All of us possess knowledge" (8:1b RSV) and walking over the consciences of other brethren? Their behavior was inexcusable. In their smug insistence that there was no harm in going to the idol feasts – since the idols themselves were nothing – they were doing an unloving and hurtful thing to those people. Paul reminded them of something we all tend to forget: "'Knowledge' puffs up, but love builds up" (8:1c RSV).

In principle, Paul could agree with the conceited

party. There really is only one God, and the idols worshipped by the heathen are non-entities. Thus the sacrifices and rites surrounding them are powerless and empty (8:4-6). The problem remained, however, that some who had been brought up in the context of heathen superstition had not yet drawn out all the logical implications entailed in the Christian doctrine of God. "Howbeit there is not in all men that knowledge: but some, being used until now to the idol, eat as of a thing sacrificed to an idol; and their conscience being weak is defiled" (8:7).

These weak brethren constitute what was called earlier the "conscientious" party at Corinth. Even though they were Christians now, some of the old thoughts and associations of idolatry lingered. They no longer worshipped those deities, but neither had they come to the point of being able to discount them totally. Workers on the mission fields today tell similar stories of people recently converted from religions involving witchcraft and voodoo. The fears are real and will require a certain amount of time to deal with and conquer.

The conceited group must have been both frightening and offensive to the conscientious party. And caught in the middle were all the confused ones. These were people who, perhaps, had seen the *intellectual* truth that idols and sacrifices to them were nothing but who were still struggling with the *emotional* implications of it. They were the ones in particular danger at Corinth.

Food does not directly affect a believer's standing with God (8:8). Since this is true, eating or not eating a particular item is a matter of indifference rather than necessity. Thus the stronger brethren at Corinth were warned against arrogance in encouraging others to violate their consciences (8:12) and even become participants in public banquets honoring idols (8:13).

"But take heed lest by any means this liberty of yours become a stumbling block to the weak" (8:9). If the weak or confused brother saw a believer eating at a public festival and participating in the ceremonies (8:10a), he might follow his example and "be emboldened to eat things sacrificed to idols" (8:10b). In such an instance, the conceited man's influence would have caused the conscientious or confused person to "stumble" (Gr, *skandalizō* = to sin, not merely take offense or object). "And thus, sinning against the brethren, and wounding their conscience when it is weak, ye sin against Christ" (8:12).

From the way this section ends, Paul indicates that he may have faced this very issue himself while at Corinth. "Wherefore, if meat causeth my brother to stumble, I will eat no flesh for evermore, that I cause not my brother to stumble" (8:13). A policy of regard for the weak brother's conscience leads to this conclusion for all Christians when facing similar situations.

Morris is correct when he observes:

> The principle laid down in this chapter is one of great practical importance. It is always easy for the strong Christian to see no harm whatever in actions which would be sin if performed by the weak. While it would not be true to say that the robust Christianity of the New Testament envisages the strong as permanently shackled by the weak, yet the strong must always act towards the weak with consideration and Christian love. In cases like the one here dealt with the strong must adapt their behaviour to the consciences of the weak. No good purpose is served by their asserting what they call their 'rights'."

Apostolic Freedom (9:1-27)

Having expressed his personal commitment to a policy of avoiding actions which would cause others to stumble, Paul uses considerable space to discuss some of the implications of this position for his apostleship. The purpose here was not boasting or self-righteous display. It was to show that he took his own counsel seriously and to allow the Corinthians to see how it worked in practical settings which are wider in scope than eating meat offered to idols. [Note: Chapter Four of this book contains several comments about 1 Cor. 9 as it relates to the work of an apostle. It would be helpful to read the relevant material from that chapter again.]

Against the possibility that some may have even been critical of him for not using all his "rights" as an apostle (9:3), Paul explains that he had deliberately chosen to forego such rights as claiming food and drink – presumably at the church's expense (9:4), marriage (9:5), or full financial support for his ministry from the people he was serving (9:6-12a).

The reason for refusing his rights was not left for anyone to guess: "But we did not use this right. On the contrary, we put up with anything rather than hinder the gospel of Christ" (9:12b NIV). All those who work full-time in any ministry to the Lord have the right to support for that work (9:13-14). Paul was not challenging others who used this right. For himself, however, he had not claimed it at Corinth (9:15-16) and was looking directly to God for his "reward" (9:17-18).

Paul, like the conceited party at Corinth, was aware that he was "free" in Christ (9:19a); Paul, unlike the conceited party, was unwilling to exercise all the rights his freedom gave him (9:19b). He had put himself under a voluntary bondage to others for the sake of reaching them with the gospel message. When among Jews, he respected their ethnic and traditional life habits to the degree that he could for the sake of winning them (9:20). He did the same among Gentiles (9:21). And when among "weak" persons like those being despised by some at Corinth, he respected their feelings (9:22). The motive was the same in every case: "And I do all things for the gospel's sake, that I may be a joint partaker thereof" (9:23). He wanted to overcome cultural barriers with people for the sake of communicating Christ to them.

Using the figure of athletic contests (9:24-27), he encourages all Christians to exercise personal self-discipline (i.e., self-denial) for the sake of the ultimate crown before us. If one foregoes a right for the sake of "becoming all things to all men" and in order to "save some," let him think of it as a small sacrifice for the sake of a much greater goal in view! If an athlete in training eats every fattening food he has the right to eat or relaxes every time he is free to do so, he is very short-sighted. He is giving up his long-range goal of victory in the games for the sake of a momentary demonstration of his right to do as he pleases. The conceited persons at Corinth were making no less serious a mistake in their behavior.

Lessons From Israel's History (10:1-13)

Just as an athlete must use self-restraint in his life, so must children of God show the same virtue in spiritual things. As an example of this principle, he calls to mind some well-known facts from Old Testament history.

God delivered Israel from bondage in Egypt (10:1), and that nation was pledged to Moses' leadership by virtue of their baptism unto him (10:2). They were nourished in the wilderness by Christ's presence to meet their needs (10:3-4). Yet "with most of them God was not well pleased: for they were overthrown in the wilderness" (10:5). Specifically, they lusted after evil things (10:6), committed idolatry (10:7), committed fornication (10:8), and otherwise made trial of the Lord's patience with them (10:9-10).

What is the relevance of all this to Corinth? These things are "examples" which warn of the possibility redeemed people face of falling away from God and eternal life (10:11-12). "Temptation" (Gr, *peirasmos* = trial) comes to the people of God in every generation, yet God will not allow any stress to come which is greater than one can bear (10:13). This is a wonderful promise to believers. God does not exempt Christians from trials. Neither does he force us to face them alone and unaided. By his grace, we can withstand and have the victory.

The situation at Corinth was not hopeless. Their trials were intense, and they had complicated them by their immature responses. But they were not abandoned by the Lord. He would provide the way for their escape from the sort of fate which befell ancient Israel.

The Lord's Table (10:14-22)

Here, then, is the practical application of all Paul has been saying on the subject: "Wherefore, my beloved, flee from idolatry" (10:14).

Eating meat which had been sacrificed to idols was not sinful in itself, for an idol is nothing. The conceited party was right on that point. The danger was, however, that they – along with the conscientious and confused brethren they could influence – might go a step further to actually join in the worship of the deities involved. Thus they would follow Israel's example of flirting with idolatry until they finally embraced and were destroyed by it!

The injunction "Flee from idolatry" is therefore to be understood as applicable to everyone at Corinth. The weak and bewildered whose consciences were being defiled through eating meat offered to idols were to avoid it altogether. So also were those whose strong consciences in the matter would otherwise have allowed them to participate without qualms. The whole church was to stay away from any and all public contexts of sacrifice and feasting in honor of pagan deities.

Just as the Lord's Supper signifies our participation with Christ (10:15-17), so does one's participation in a sacrifice denote communion with the deity whose altar receives the sacrifice. This was true of fleshly Israel and Yahweh (10:18); it was true of pagan sacrifice and their deities (i.e., demons) at Corinth (10:19-20a). "And I would not that ye should have communion with demons. Ye cannot drink the cup of the Lord, and the cup of demons: ye cannot partake of the table of the Lord, and of the table of demons" (10:20b-21).

In the *public* ceremonies involving pagan deities, sacrifices, and sacrificial meats, Christians were to be conspicuously absent at Corinth! They were not to "provoke the Lord to jealousy" (10:22a) as Israel had done in the wilderness. They were not "stronger than he" (10:22b) and could not withstand his wrath any more successfully than the fallen Israelites had.

The matter is settled, then, for situations involving public participation in idol feasts. But what of those *private* settings where meat once offered in sacrifice might be purchased at the butcher shops in Corinth?

Liberty and Love (10:23-11:1)

Referring back to the principle enunciated earlier in chapter eight (i.e., eating food sacrificed to idols is neither intrinsically good nor evil), Paul now relates that truth to the fundamental regulator of all Christian conduct – love. Yes, the activity itself is "lawful"; but the loving questions of what is "expedient" (i.e., beneficial) and what will "edify" (i.e., be constructive) also need to be raised (10:23). Why? "Let no man seek his own, but each his neighbor's good" (10:24).

Anything sold in the meat market ("shambles"

in KJV and ASV) has lost its association with idol worship – unlike meat eaten on the site of the idol temple or in the context of an idol festival – and can be eaten by Christians (10:25-26). Thus when a Christian is invited to dine with an unbeliever in the context of a private (i.e., non-sacrificial) meal, he should feel free to go and need not inquire about what he is served (10:27). On the other hand, if one's host presents the meat as having been offered in sacrifice and thus consecrated to a pagan deity, he should decline it (10:28-29a). He declines for the sake of any brother in Christ who might not understand his "liberty" and whose conscience would be offended in the matter (10:29b-30). Liberty is thus subordinated to love. Christ is honored, and the weak brother is protected.

In everything done by Christians, even the things we would consider so small and insignificant, the primary consideration must be "the glory of God" (10:31). This implies a vigilant concern for one's influence over all others who may observe our behavior – both non-Christians and other members of the body of Christ (10:32-33). Since Paul had been careful to practice this very thing among them, he could encourage the Corinthians to imitate his example in the matter (11:1).

Exercising Our Freedoms

Christian maturity does not allow the view that each believer is "an island unto himself" who lives by the every-man-for-himself principle. Mature faith looks to the needs of those who are new in the faith and seeks to ground and establish them. It does not ride roughshod over their scruples and weaknesses.

No one should attempt to force a brother or sister to violate his or her conscience in any matter. To do so would be to place a stumbling block (i.e., snare or trap) in that person's path.

Yet we must remember that Paul did *not* say that Christians can do only those things to which no one raises an objection. To interpret what he said in so broad a fashion would mean that no one could do anything. Some brother or sister objects to everything – from eating on church property to having more than one container on the communion table to sending greeting cards or exchanging gifts at Christmas. We must never do anything that will entice or coerce another person into sin; we may do an almost infinite number of right things that do not implicate others.

Take, as modern examples, Christmas observance and social drinking.

Some Christians have conscientious objections against singing "Joy to the World" on December 25, sending Christmas cards (especially if they have a religious motif), or otherwise attaching any spiritual significance to this holiday. Practically everyone knows that we are in the dark about the precise date of the Savior's birth and that Christmas is not an appointed celebration which is commanded in the New Testament. But one would be hard pressed to argue that praise to heaven for the entrance of the Son of God into human history would be wrong on any day of the year –including December 25.

Paul addressed this issue of observing non-essential "holy days" in Romans 14. He said to let each believer do as he wished in the matter and for none to judge his brother (Rom. 14:5-7). So do as you please in the matter.

Social drinking seems to be quite different in nature from sending Christmas cards. Although one can point out that there is nothing intrinsically evil about alcohol (otherwise it would be sinful to use it even in medicines) and that Jesus and his disciples lived in a culture where wine was a common table drink for everyone, the principle of love for one's brother causes most Christians to adopt a posture of total abstinence from alcohol. Alcohol is associated with so many problems in our culture (e.g., accidents, marital failure, child abuse, etc.) that a mature believer would never – even if he can "handle his liquor" – want to be guilty of encouraging someone else to use a product that holds so many potentials for evil.

The former issue is much more personal to each individual and does not lure others into spiritual danger; the latter one has far too many implications to defend as a private choice which has no implications for others' behavior.

Conclusion

Only a short list of things are declared in the New Testament to be "works of the flesh" and therefore wrong in and of themselves. But to conclude from this, as some had at Corinth, that "all things are permissible" would be to overstep the bounds of Christian reason and conduct. Some things that are lawful of themselves may nevertheless be neither helpful nor beneficial to others.

Love for others and a genuine concern to do nothing which would cause weaker Christians to stumble or hinder our efforts to bring non-Christians to faith will produce a lifestyle very different from that of the conceited group at Corinth.

Study Questions

1. Identify the three positions being taken at Corinth on the matter of eating meat sacrificed to idols.

2. What was the harm being done by the "conceited party" at Corinth? Discuss 1 Cor. 8:1c in relation to the conduct of those people.

3. What modern parallels can you think of for the "conscientious party" at Corinth?

4. Did Paul teach that one must forego anything to which some other brother objects? What did he say? What is it to cause another to "stumble"?

5. Why had Paul not claimed all the rights he was entitled to at Corinth? How did his example speak to the situation he was writing about in this epistle?

6. Paul used a metaphor from athletic contests in 1 Cor. 9:24-27. What was the point of its use? Why would it have been meaningful to the people at Corinth?

7. Explain the promise of 1 Cor. 10:13. What is the practical meaning of this promise to struggling Christians in every age?

8. What does the Lord's Supper mean concerning one's union with Christ? Why would eating that feast rule out one's participation in the idol feasts at Corinth?

9. Put the meaning of 1 Cor. 10:23-24 into your own words. Show that the principle involved extends far beyond the particular issue Paul was addressing here.

10. What are your own attitudes toward Christmas observance and social drinking? Are these legitimate examples of modern-day concerns which parallel some of the things which were going on at Corinth?

9/ Respecting God's Order of Things

1 Cor. 11:2-34

The eleventh chapter of 1 Corinthians deals with *worship*. More specifically, it deals with a pair of abuses in worship which were hindering the spiritual life of the church at Corinth.

First, some of the "liberated" women of the church were disregarding custom and propriety in their society by failing to wear veils in public assemblies. Second, the church was making a farce of the Lord's Supper by turning it into a banquet.

In this chapter, Paul pleads for Christians to respect the divine order in all relationships – particularly in worship settings. There are insights here which children of God still need very desperately.

The Beauty of Worship

The significant day of worship for Christians is the Lord's Day, Sunday. Paul will later refer to the customary assembly day at Corinth and will identify it as "the first day of the week" (1 Cor. 16:2). This is the day on which Jesus arose from the dead (Mark 16:9). It is the day when the Holy Spirit came on the apostles in Jerusalem and caused the church to be established among men (Acts 2).

Besides the references to worship among the Christians in the New Testament, there are several early descriptions of their practices in non-biblical literature. One of the most moving is found in the correspondence of a Roman bureaucrat with his emperor. Around A.D. 111 Pliny was appointed to serve as imperial legate of the province of Bithynia in Asia Minor. While filling his post, he carried on an amazing exchange of letters with the imperial court. He wrote long letters which give the details of situations facing him and asked help from his emperor in deciding what to do in response to them. Writing to Trajan (emperor A.D. 98-117), he explained his problem in conducting trials of persons accused of being Christians. It contains a beautiful description of the worship Christians conducted.

> They maintained that their fault or error amounted to nothing more than this: they were in the habit of meeting on a certain fixed day before sunrise and singing in alternate verses a hymn to Christ as divine, and binding themselves with an oath not to commit any crime, but to abstain from all acts of theft, robbery, and adultery, from breaches of faith, from repudiating a trust when called on to honor it. (Pliny, *Epistles*. 10. 96.)

Local churches should be worshipping communities. God both deserves and demands worship from his people (John 4:24), and the church is that consecrated body of people which is authorized to serve as a priesthood for the offering up of sincere worship (1 Pet. 2:9).

Each part of the church's worship meets some vital need in believers' spiritual lives. Study of the

Word of God nurtures faith (Rom. 10:17). Singing exalts Father, Son, and Holy Spirit and exhorts Christians to faithfulness (Col. 3:16). Giving of our money to finance the work of the church makes us partners in God's work and keeps our hearts from selfishness (2 Cor. 9:7). United prayer gives Christians power with God in the assurance that he will hear and answer our prayers (Jas. 5:16b). The Lord's Supper takes us back to the central event of our faith and focuses our hearts on the atonement (1 Cor. 10:16-17).

Because worship meets urgent needs in our spiritual lives, Christians are commanded not to forsake assembling together for the experience (Heb. 10:25).

At Corinth, however, worship was probably a negative experience in the spiritual lives of most believers. The abuses of this beautiful exercise were making the body less attractive to outsiders and less effective in trying to share the gospel with them. Some things had to be changed quickly.

Examining the Text

Accustomed as most of us are to worship which is sober and orderly, it is unlikely that we can even visualize what was happening at Corinth. For one thing, there was the excitement of the exercise of spiritual gifts (cf. 1 Cor. 12-14). Then there was the occasional sight of a woman casting aside her veil and speaking publicly to pray or prophesy. And the Lord's Supper was observed not as a solemn commemoration of Christ's death but as a time for display, eating, and drinking on the order of a pagan banquet.

Women, Veils, and Propriety (11:2-16)

There is a great deal we do not know about the veil at Corinth and in the Greco-Roman world at

large in the first century. For one thing, we could
wish we had the detailed question to which Paul
was replying. For another, we need more data on
the veil generally in order to arrive at fixed conclusions. We know, for example, that heavy veils were
worn by women at Jerusalem and throughout the
East generally. But there is good evidence to the
effect that Greek and Roman women did not always
follow the same custom.

Paul begins by praising the Corinthians for their
general fidelity to "the traditions" he had delivered
them (11:2). By this term we are likely to understand the authoritative teaching received from the
Lord rather than mere social custom (cf. 2 Thess.
2:15). He will shortly demonstrate that there are
sometimes direct connections between divine de-
liverances and proper respect for human customs
in a particular situation.

The apostle called attention to the order of authority and submission which heaven has established and insisted that the Christian women at
Corinth respect that order. "But I would have you
know, that the head of every man is Christ; and the
head of the woman is the man; and the head of
Christ is God" (11:3). Christ is God's equal in nature and essence (cf. Phil. 2:5-6); he became subordinate to the Godhead for the sake of a particular
function. Woman is man's equal in nature and essence (cf. Gal. 3:28); she is subordinate to him for
the sake of a particular function. Women are to be
subject to men and to respect the leadership God
has given them in the affairs of the church.

The appropriate signs of their acceptance of God's
order of authority at Corinth would be for the man
to keep his head uncovered (11:4) and for the woman
to wear a veil or shawl over her head in worship
settings (11:5a). For men to repudiate their authority in relation to women by adopting the veil
would have been wrong; for women to challenge

male leadership by refusing the veil would have been equally improper.

A traditional interpretation of verse 5 holds that a woman was permitted to pray and/or prophesy before the church at Corinth in at least one circumstance (i.e., when she had a spiritual gift) – so long as she wore her veil while doing so. Those holding this view usually go on to say that, since there are no similar gifts today, this verse gives no authority for women to pray or preach before the church today. It is hard to reconcile this interpretation with what is going to be said later in the epistle (1 Cor. 14:34).

An alternate view holds that this verse forbids the woman to speak at all to lead assemblies in worship. [Cf. Noel Weeks, "Of Silence and Head Covering," *Westminster Theological Journal* 35 (Fall 1972): 21-27.] On this view, Paul's argument here is a powerful *reductio ad absurdum*. Prayer and prophecy are functions which unquestionably involve authority when exercised in relation to others. On the other hand, the covering of one's head with a veil at Corinth signified subordination to others. One or the other of these actions may be performed by an individual but not both simultaneously, for one is the negation of the other. Which should the woman do? Since the removal of the veil was equivalent to being a shaved-headed woman (i.e., a loose woman, probably a prostitute) and since being a shaved woman is a disgraceful thing (10:6), the only proper thing for a Christian woman at Corinth to do was to retain her veil and to forego prayer and prophesying before the church.

Regardless of the particular application at Corinth, there is a trans-cultural principle about woman's subordination to man in the church which must be taught and respected under all circumstances. Women may teach by godly example (1 Pet. 3:1-2). They may assist men in teaching individuals in private settings (e.g., home studies, cf. Acts 18:26) so long as they do not assume effective authority over their husbands or other males being instructed. They may teach children and other women in either private or public settings (Tit. 2:3; Acts 16:13).

The woman's submission to her husband or to leaders in the church is not a denigration of her status before God. To the contrary, by respecting those relationships she is demonstrating her obedience to God. The respect both men and women have for God's order of things on this point is not a tool for suppressing women or a cruel demeaning of their individuality. It is humble acknowledgment of the context God has designed for her as man's complement and helper in all things.

Complementary roles of leadership and submission are necessary both for maintaining marriages and building churches. As women look to Christ, they find a perfect model of willing submission. His absolute submission (cf. Luke 22:42) in no way diminished his personhood, worth, or dignity.

Man was prior to woman in creation (10:7a) and is "the image and glory of God"; thus he honors God by being in submission to him. Woman was created from and for man and is "the glory of the man" (10:7b-9); thus she honors her relationship with him by being in submission to his leadership (10:10).

Lest anything said to this point be taken as being negative toward woman, Paul immediately affirms her worth and mutual dependence with man on God (10:11-12). There is genuine partnership between the sexes, and it would be wrong for men to treat women with disrespect or abuse (cf. Eph. 5:21-30).

His final argument against the rejection of the veil at Corinth is essentially a sociological one. He appeals to their own sense of propriety in light of community practice (10:13) and nature (10:14-15). Paul's point here seems to be that "nature" (i.e., both the created order and general custom) recognizes a distinction between the sexes. It is not the business of Christians to repudiate and challenge that natural distinction in their conduct. Barrett thinks there is a likelihood that this part of the text is set against the "horror" of homosexuality and its perversion of natural sexual distinctions. The point is not to prescribe precise hair lengths or clothing styles but to uphold the necessity of clear role distinctions between the sexes.

Against the possibility that someone might reject his counsel on the veil and related behavior, Paul states flatly: "If any one is disposed to be contentious, we recognize no other practice, nor do the churches of God" (11:16 RSV).

Depreciating The Lord's Supper (11:17-34)

Having commended them earlier in the chapter for their general regard for his instructions to them (cf. 11:2), the apostle looked at the Corinthians' behavior in the Lord's Supper and wrote: "But in the following instructions I do not commend you ... Shall I commend you in this? No, I will not" (11:17a, 22b RSV).

Their manner of participating in that holy feast was doing them more harm than good (11:17b) because of their misbehavior. They were eating in the context of "divisions" (11:18) and "factions" (11:19). These were not the ones of 1 Cor. 1:10ff but appear to have been purely social. The wealthy members were discriminating against the poorer ones; some were banqueting while others were unable to bring anything to the table (11:20-21). "Eat your common meals at home or in some other appropriate social setting," he told them, "and allow the Lord's Supper to remain the simple, spiritual meal the Savior intended it to be" (11:22).

Paul thought it wise simply to refresh their memories about the event by retelling the circumstance of Jesus' instructions about it. "For I received of the Lord that which also I delivered unto you, that the Lord Jesus in the night in which he was betrayed took bread; and when he had given thanks, he brake it, and said, This is my body, which is for you: this do in remembrance of me. In like manner also the cup, after supper, saying, This cup is the new covenant in my blood: this do, as often as ye drink it, in remembrance of me" (11:23-25; cf. Matt. 26:26-29; Mark 14:22-25; Luke 22:14-20).

It was a simple and solemn observance. How inappropriate was the Corinthian manner of observance! The simple unleavened bread and wine were symbols of the body and blood of the Son of God. In abandoning that simplicity, the people at Corinth were making it increasingly unlikely that they would continue tinue to discern its significance. As some turned the event into a display of their wealth and gorged themselves with food, others resented their showiness and despaired of matching their bounty. Each group was focusing attention on itself rather than the Lord.

Paul's comment on the supper was this: "For as often as ye eat this bread, and drink the cup, ye proclaim the Lord's death till he come" (11:26). As Robertson and Plummer observe, this meal is intended to be "an *acted* sermon, an *acted* proclamation of the death which it commemorates." This purpose is not to be abandoned so long as the Lord remains in heaven awaiting the Second Coming. Yet it had already been left behind at Corinth. There was no remembrance, no proclamation, no anticipation. Instead there was selfishness, rivalry, and chaos. The result was spiritual illness and death (11:30) – conditions which could be corrected by their own self-examination (i.e., "judgment") and correction of these abuses (11:31-32).

The means to self-examination and correction were specified: "Wherefore whosoever shall eat the bread or drink the cup of the Lord in an unworthy manner, shall be guilty of the body and the blood of the Lord. But let a man prove himself, and so let him eat of the bread, and drink of the cup. For he that eateth and drinketh, eateth and drinketh judgment unto himself, if he discern not the body" (11:27-29).

One participates in the Lord's Supper "in an unworthy manner" through irreverence and thoughtlessness of the sort which was characteristic at Corinth. One must come to this meal with serious purpose, remembering with gratitude the sacrifice which saved him and examining his present walk with the Lord in view of his return. Please note that Paul does not bar unworthy *persons* from this supper, for that would keep all of us away from the table of the Lord. He bids all Christians – unworthy as we are of the sacrifice being commemorated – to come to the table of the Lord in a worthy (i.e., appropriate, fitting) *manner of participation*. One eats and drinks "judgment unto himself" by eating in the manner described earlier in verses 18-22.

Thus the apostle, with agony over these people which shows in every line, pleaded for them to tend to their physical hunger outside the context of worship observances so their spiritual hunger could be satisfied in their assemblies (11:33-34). To follow this procedure would be to respect God's order of things. Both needs are legitimate, and God has provided a circumstance of satisfaction for each.

Conclusion

Worship should be a special experience for the family of God. People who love the Lord Jesus assemble to praise him and encourage one another.

Respecting God's order of things from creation through the atonement to their daily lives as Christians, these people reflect his holiness to the communities in which they are found. Whenever they forget God's order of things, their worship can become an unspiritual exercise which does disservice to the body and drives unbelievers away.

The veil at Corinth was a cultural phenomenon of that time and place. No one is offended today when a woman in New York, Nashville, or San Francisco goes into a public place without a shawl over her head. Thus we do not import the veil from that ancient culture into ours – any more than we import the "holy kiss" (Rom. 16:16) of that time to our own. We do, however, respect the principle involved and honor equivalent cultural phenomena (e.g., appropriate concessions by an American Christian traveling or working in the Far East to that culture). And we must certainly insist on the observance of God's ordained relationships of leadership and submission between men and women in family and church affairs.

Our worship must also give appropriate emphasis and serious purpose to the Lord's Supper. We can no more turn it into a "church picnic" today then they did then without reaping the same horrible consequences. We have houses to sleep and eat in; we can have church picnics and fellowship dinners to promote a sense of community within the body. But these family and social activities are different in nature and time than the simple event of commemorating the death of the Son of God with bread and wine.

Spiritual growth at Corinth depended largely on the saints there making their worship into a truly spiritual experience. The same is true for Christians of all times and places.

Study Questions

1. Reflect on Pliny's description of Christian worship. How could such activities have been considered dangerous to the Roman state? Why had Christianity become an illegal religion by his time?

2. Show how each element of the church's worship meets specific spiritual needs in the lives of believers.

3. What was the general significance of the wearing of a veil by women in the ancient world? Where is such a practice still perpetuated?

4. Why would it have been wrong for men to wear a veil during worship at Corinth? Why would it have been wrong for women to reject the veil?

5. 1 Cor. 11:5 is a difficult verse to interpret. Which of the two views presented in the chapter seems more reasonable to you? Is there a third alternative you could offer?

6. What limitations does the Bible place on the public teaching role of women? What opportunities for teaching by women are established in Scripture?

7. In what ways could the talents and energies of women be employed more effectively in the work of the church today?

8. Try to visualize and describe the circumstances surrounding the eating of the Lord's Supper at Corinth. What were the "divisions" and "factions" which accompanied the event? In what ways do we sometimes degrade the Lord's Supper?

9. What sort of self-examination is appropriate for Christians when we gather to eat the Lord's Supper?

10. Explain the meaning of 1 Cor. 11:27. Have you ever known people to refuse to eat the Lord's Supper because they felt themselves "unworthy"? Is this the meaning of Paul's statement?

10/ Spiritual Gifts in the Early Church

1 Cor. 12:1 –14:40

The Christian Era was ushered in when the Holy Spirit came on the apostles in fulfillment of Jesus' promise to endue them with power from on high (Acts 1:8; 2:1-4). The Spirit aided the Twelve and certain other specially chosen evangelists as they preached, wrote, and confirmed the gospel. "This salvation, which was first announced by the Lord, was confirmed to us by those who heard him. God also testified to it by signs, wonders and various miracles, and gifts of the Holy Spirit distributed according to his will" (Heb. 2:3b-4 NIV).

In the epistle we are studying, Paul has already had several important things to say about the Holy Spirit. In particular, he has declared the church to be the place of the Spirit's abode among men (1 Cor. 3:16). He has argued for sexual purity on the basis of the fact that the bodies of individual believers are temples of the Holy Spirit who indwells them (1 Cor. 6:18-20).

At this point in the letter to Corinth, Paul addresses the subject of supernatural gifts among men. The Holy Spirit had granted certain miraculous powers to different Christians in that church. The purpose of the gifts was to strengthen the body (14:12, 26). They had served an opposite end at Corinth. The gifts were from God and legitimate; they were not demonic imitations of spiritual gifts or fraudulent claims by lying men. They were genuine! But in the context of the division, jealousy, and unspiritual attitudes of that church, they had become simply another point of contention and strife.

They had taken their charismatic gifts to be ends in themselves. To the contrary, Paul insisted, they were means to the larger end of building up the body. Without love, however, these beautiful gifts had become liabilities to the church rather than assets. What had happened at Corinth was something akin to giving gold nuggets the size of snowballs to those saints – only to watch them use their gifts as snowball-type weapons to hurl at one another! It was the irresponsible behavior of children!

Focus: The Holy Spirit

Although we sometimes use the neuter pronoun "it" of the Holy Spirit, the correct view is to ascribe divine personality to him. He is a full-fledged member of the divine family (i.e., the Godhead, Deity). God the Father, God the Word, and God the Holy Spirit are alike in their eternality, omniscience, omnipotence, and other perfect attributes. These three separate personalities are nevertheless *one God* (Deut.6:4). Their oneness is not that of numerical sequence (i.e., 0, 1, 2, etc.) but of a state of unity. Just as husband and wife are "one" in marriage (Gen. 2:24) and just as Paul and Apollos had been "one" in their work at Corinth (1 Cor. 3:6-8), so are Father, Son, and Holy Spirit *one* in their communion and function.

In Old Testament times, the Holy Spirit gave visions, dreams, and the power to prophesy to certain individuals (2 Pet. 1:21). He also equipped people for special tasks of ministry they were to perform: wisdom to rulers (Num. 11:16-17, 25-29; 1 Sam. 10:10; 16:13), courage and strength to deliverers (Judg. 3:10; 13:24-25), and even skill for artistic work to be done for the tabernacle (Ex. 31:1-5; 35:30-35).

The New Testament contains many more direct references to the Holy Spirit and his work. He played a primary role in the incarnation of Jesus (Matt. 1:20) and descended on Jesus as a dove at his baptism (Mark 11:10). There are more than 60 references to the Spirit in the Gospels. It is in Acts and the New Testament epistles, however, that so much is told of his specific workings in the plan of God to bring all men to salvation.

The most frequent word for the miraculous gifts of the Spirit in the New Testament is *charisma* — from which we derive our English word "charismatic." It is usually translated "spiritual gift." The primary meaning of the word is "a gift (freely and graciously given), a favor bestowed" (Arndt and Gingrich). Although the word is used to refer to such non-miraculous things as the bestowing of salvation (cf. Rom. 5:15-16; 6:23) and the impartation of knowledge through human instruction (cf. Rom. 1:11), it is sometimes used by Paul in a technical sense to denote "extraordinary powers, distinguishing certain Christians and enabling them to serve the church of Christ, the reception of which is due to the power of divine grace operating in their souls by the Holy Spirit" (Thayer).

A second word used to refer to such gifts is *pneumatikos*. Although this word can also refer to things other than miraculous gifts, when it is used with the definite article (*ta pneumatika,* cf. 1 Cor. 12 – 14), its translation is "spiritual gifts" and its meaning is the same as the technical definition given above for *charismata*.

We may say, then, that spiritual gifts were those supernatural powers and abilities given certain God-chosen individuals which would enable them to perform special acts of spiritual service in the establishment and spread of the church.

Focus: The Text

The most extended discussion of spiritual gifts at any one place in the New Testament is our text for this study. We may outline this material in broad form as follows: confusion over spiritual gifts (ch. 12), a better way (ch. 13), and some guidelines for order (ch. 14).

A fundamental misunderstanding of the nature of the Christian life was at the root of the problems over spiritual gifts at Corinth. Immature Christians had taken the presence of the Spirit's supernatural powers among them as proof both of their justification and perfection in Christ. It was neither! Let us see how the apostle addressed the situation.

Confusion Over Spiritual Gifts (12:1-31)

The proof of one's justification before God is not charismatic gifts. It is the daily acknowledgment of Jesus Christ as Lord in a believer's life. The saints at Corinth had once served "dumb idols" (12:2) and were thereby implicated in demonic evil (cf. 1 Cor. 10:21). Now, however, they had been brought to the light through the revelation of Jesus through God's Spirit. "Wherefore I make known unto you, that no man speaking in the Spirit of God saith, Jesus is anathema; and no man can say, Jesus is Lord, but in the Holy Spirit" (12:3).

The Spirit's most important ministry is pointing people to Jesus. He shows the things of this world to be empty and condemned (John 16:8-10); he reveals Jesus to those who will receive his word (John 16:12-15). He exalts Jesus in his redemptive role and helps believers live consistently with our holy calling. To see only his supernatural gifts, to covet and abuse them, or to confuse and disrupt the life of the church over them is to miss the point of his ministry.

The one God – Father, Son, and Holy Spirit – distributed gifts at Corinth (12:4-6). Their fundamental unity should have been served by those gifts and not frustrated. "Now to each man the manifestation of the Spirit is given for the common good" (12:7). But "the common good" (i.e., building up the entire body) was not being served because of their strife, division, and jealousy. There has to be a better way.

Paul lists a total of nine spiritual gifts – each of which was apparently present among the Corinthians: the word of wisdom, the word of knowledge, faith, gifts of healing, workings of miracles, prophecy, discerning of spirits, tongues, and the interpretation of tongues (12:8-11). Some would enlarge the total list of spiritual gifts to 16 by adding apostleship, teaching, giving assistance, governing (cf. 12:28), being an evangelist, being a pastor (cf. Eph. 4:11), and liberality (cf. Rom. 12:8). It seems just as reasonable, however, to think the longer list is produced by separating the abilities listed in 1 Cor. 12:8-11 from their exercise through specific individuals. For example, teaching is simply the exercise of the gift of prophecy and/or knowledge.

There is no evidence either that every Christian at Corinth has a charismatic gift or that a believer with one gift could equally claim and demonstrate the other eight (cf. 12:30). It also seems obvious that there was no one gift (e.g., tongues) that all believers possessed as evidence of their justification (cf. 12:19).

In the context of the divisions among his original readers, Paul's primary point here is not to list or explain the gifts. His point is to stress unity among the saints and to encourage the use of their gifts for mutual benefit. The body of Christ is a unit (12:12) by virtue of the fact that every member has been placed in it through baptism and each has been given the same Spirit to indwell him (12:23; cf. Acts 2:38). No one part of this interdependent body can see itself – with justification – as aloof from and without need of the other parts of the body (12:14-26).

The church really is similar to a human body. Differences exist among the various parts. Diversity of function is not only to be allowed but encouraged. The unity of the body does not equate with bland sameness. Each member has his or her own unique personhood. God may endow one with this gift or ministry and another with a different one. But there is *one body,* and everything fits together for its benefit in God's plan. Verse 27 seems almost to jump from the page: "Now you are the body of Christ, and each one of you is a part of it." Stop boasting of your gift! Quit discounting your brother's! All you Corinthian Christians are members of the same body.

Paul insisted that God never intended for spiritual gifts to be the proof of salvation (12:28-30). Indeed, he has already said in verse 3 that faith in Jesus as Lord – not possession of particular charismatic powers – is the evidence of sanctification and of the presence of the Holy Spirit. Their distorted view of spiritual gifts was threatening their daily life under Jesus' Lordship. *There has to be a better way!* Indeed, there was "the most excellent way" of love – whether one had a spiritual gift or not – which Paul wanted his readers to learn and exhibit.

A Better Way (13:1-13)

The people at Corinth were pointing to their supernatural gifts as proof that God was pleased with them, that they were filled, rich, and reigning (cf 1 Cor. 4:8). What egotism! What misapprehension of the nature of the religion they had embraced under Paul's instruction!

Speaking in tongues, supernatural knowledge, miracle-working faith, sacrificial liberality, even martyrdom – all are meaningless without love (13:1-3).

Love (Gr, *agapē*) is more than a word to be used among God's people. It is not an emotion which comes and goes independently of our wills. It is a pattern of behavior which has been revealed by God and can be learned by Christians.

It takes a minimal amount of creative imagination to read the following words and see how each quality of love identified by Paul is a specific corrective for the Corinthian problems: "Love is patient, love is kind. It does not envy, it does not boast, it is not proud. It is not rude, it is not self-seeking, it is not easily angered, it keeps no record of wrongs. Love does not delight in evil but rejoices in the truth. It always protects, always trusts, always hopes, always perseveres" (13:4-7 NIV).

Love is a permanent and universal evidence of the presence of the Spirit of God in believers (13:8a; cf. Gal. 5:21-23). Charismatic gifts of prophecy, tongues, and knowledge were temporary and particular to specific individuals (13:8b-12). They were destined to be done away and to cease. So long as the knowledge and prophecy necessary to reveal God's will to mankind were "in part" (i.e., incomplete, imperfect), the gifts would be in evidence. When they were "perfect" (i.e., in full, completed), the gifts would be withdrawn. Love will always remain. "But now abideth faith, hope, love, these three; and the greatest of these is love" (13:13). Love is "greatest" of these three because it is the one which activates the other two and causes them to function properly and for the benefit of the whole body.

Some Guidelines For Order (14:1-40)

Now it is time for Paul to apply all that has been said about gifts, their relative importance, and their use in loving concern for the entire body to the specific problems at Corinth.

First, love must be the governing principle in the use of gifts. This would mean, for example, that prophecy would be more desirable than tongues at Corinth (14:1). Why? While speaking in tongues must have been an impressive and showy phenomenon – thus a potential source of pride in its possessor – it was not particularly profitable for those who witnessed it. Unless an interpreter translated what had been said for the hearers, no one understood what the man was saying except God – not even the man himself (14:2-4a). On the other hand, prophecy (i.e., inspired preaching) benefits everyone (14:4b). Speaking in tongues has a similar benefit only when it is immediately interpreted; in such a case, it becomes inspired preaching, too (14:5).

Vivid illustrations of his point are given which show that glossalalia (i.e., speaking in tongues) could become nothing more than noise without meaning (14:6-12a). A non-understood message in a language foreign to everyone present might have been awe-inspiring. It would *not* have been very helpful! "Since you are eager to have spiritual gifts, try to excel in gifts that build up the church" (14:12b NIV).

With love governing the gifts, anyone with the gift of tongues should pray for the gift of interpretation to be in evidence as well (14:13-21). Without interpretations for the things revealed through glossalalia, unbelievers present for the service would not only go away unenlightened but possibly ridiculing the whole scene as an exercise in madness (14:22-23). The same unbeliever present when prophecy was being given had the greater likelihood of being convicted of his own sinfulness and feeling the need to know the God of whom he had learned through the preaching he had heard (14:24-25).

Second, the Corinthians were henceforth to observe some specific rules about the exercise of spiritual gifts. Few gifts were to be displayed at any one service (i.e., only two or three) and then only one at a time rather than in chaotic competition for attention (14:26-27). If no one with the gift of interpretation was present, tongues-speakers were to be silent (14:28).

Third, all possessors of charismatic gifts were to acknowledge that their gifts were not beyond their ability to control. Otherwise how could they obey Paul's command about restraint and silence under certain conditions? (14:29-32). The public life of the church must not be an exercise in confusion (14:33a).

Fourth, in services where these gifts were being employed, women were forbidden to speak out (14:33b-35). The people at Corinth were not to create different guidelines for female participation in these services than Paul and the other apostles had established among the other churches (14:36). [See the comments in Chapter Nine about women, veils, and speaking in the assemblies of the church.]

Fifth, everything said by anyone who claimed to be a prophet, tongues-speaker, or interpreter at Corinth was to be studied and evaluated in light of the written Word of God and previous instruction from apostles such as Paul. "If anybody thinks he is a prophet or spiritually gifted, let him acknowledge that what I am writing to you is the Lord's command. If he ignores this, he himself will be

ignored" (14:37-38). Spiritual gifts have never been
intended to denigrate or set aside the written Word.
Whenever anything is claimed or done in the name
of "charismatic leadership" which is inconsistent
with that Word, it must be discounted and resisted.
The revelation given through the apostles and their
closest associates remains normative for all times
and all situations (cf. 1 John 4:6).

Paul closed this matter with a disclaimer. He
was not opposing the use of whatever gifts God had
distributed at Corinth (14:39). He was only insisting that they be used in a fitting and profitable
manner (14:40).

Focus: Spiritual Gifts Today

The miraculous gifts given to people by the Holy
Spirit in the church's early days were designed to
serve three primary purposes.

First, spiritual gifts were the means of communicating the message of Christ to the world without
error. It was the "Spirit of Christ in them" who
enabled the Old Testament prophets to foresee the
coming of the Messiah (1 Pet. 1:11); it was the same
"Holy Spirit sent forth from heaven" who caused
the gospel to be preached among all men after Jesus appeared (1 Pet. 1:12).

Second, miraculous powers were used to confirm
the gospel as it was being revealed. The men who
went from place to place preaching the message of
Christ needed some sort of credentials for their
Spirit-given ministry. The Holy Spirit gave them
gifts which would not only enable these spokesmen
to reveal the divine will but also to confirm it as
from God and authoritative (cf. Acts 14:3).

Three, charismatic gifts enabled the infant church
to perform certain of its great tasks in its formative
years. The gift of tongues allowed the Word to be
preached in places where the native language(s) of

the apostles were not known; the ability to distinguish spirits (i.e., to judge between true and false prophets) protected the church from doctrinal corruptions; and so with each of the special powers.

Today these purposes are achieved through the work of the Holy Spirit through the written Word and his non-miraculous indwelling of the saved. (1) The complete gospel is in our possession in the form of the written Word. (2) It stands confirmed, and the repetition of the original signs of the Spirit would not convince the skeptics who disallow the record of them in an inerrant Scripture. (3) We are able to be equipped unto every good work God wants done in this world through the combining of our consecrated energies under the authority of the Word of God (cf. 2 Tim. 3:16-17).

Someone objects: "But miracles before men's eyes today could do what the Bible cannot do for them!" While I understand the genuine sincerity of such an objection, the fact of the matter is that the written Word is more important than charismatic gifts. For one thing, Paul said in the text studied in this section of his epistle (14:37-38) that the written Word is normative over alleged charismatic gifts. For another, Peter spoke of his astounding experience in witnessing the Transfiguration of Jesus and said: "And we have the prophetic word made more sure. You will do well to pay attention to this as to a lamp shining in a dark place ... because no prophecy ever came by the impulse of man, but men moved by the Holy Spirit spoke from God" (2 Pet. 1:19-21 RSV).

Jesus himself underscored this truth of the priority of God's written Word over personal experiences in the story of the rich man and Lazarus. From his torment in Hades, the rich man pleaded with Abraham to send Lazarus back to earth to warn his brothers. "But Abraham saith, They have Moses and the prophets; let them hear them. And he said, Nay, father Abraham: but if one go to them from the dead, they will repent. And he said unto him, If they hear not Moses and the prophets, neither will they be persuaded, if one rise from the dead" (Luke 16:27-31).

Faith has to rest on something more stable than miraculous phenomena which one has witnessed. Alleged exorcisms, healings, and visions are stock in trade for witch doctors and anti-Christian occultists. Thus heaven has been sparing in its use of miracles in a few crucial contexts of revelation. Beyond those brief episodes, faith has been built on the written and preached word.

When an eagle bears her young, she builds a nest high in the mountains. There she hatches and nourishes her babies. When the time comes that the fledglings are ready to fly, she destroys the nest. The temporary place of nourishment and care is dismantled, and the young birds are forced to fly. Today God wants us to soar on the wings of faith, but our faith "comes by hearing the message, and the message is heard through the word of Christ" (Rom. 10:17).

Conclusion

By the gracious Spirit of God, the church was founded and sustained in the temporary "nest" of spiritual gifts. Even in those earliest and most exciting of times, the Spirit's first function was to exalt Christ, promote love among believers, and foster the working of the church for the common benefit of all the saints.

Today the "nest" is dismantled. But the Spirit of God is still present to perform his primary work in the life of the church (cf. Rom. 8:1-17; Eph. 4:11-19). He exalts Christ through the Word, promotes love among Christians as a fruit of his presence in our lives, and blesses the work of the church for the common good of all its people.

Study Questions

1. What was the fundamental purpose behind the giving of supernatural powers to Christians in the earliest days of the church? Why was that purpose being defeated at Corinth?

2. Give a brief summary of the work of the Holy Spirit in the Old Testament. How does that ministry compare with his work in the New Testament?

3. What does the term "spiritual gift" refer to? Define the following terms: charismatic, glossalalia, and miracle.

4. Identify and give a description of the nine spiritual gifts which Paul enumerated in 1 Cor. 12.

5. Paul's primary point in chapter 12 seems to have been an emphasis on *unity in the body* the use of spiritual gifts to support that unity. How does this theme relate to the overall content of the epistle?

6. Why are all other gifts and powers useless in service to Christ when they are divorced from *love*?

7. Contrast the temporary nature of spiritual gifts with the abiding nature of love. When did supernatural gifts of the Holy Spirit cease to be available to mankind?

8. Discuss each of the "guidelines for order" which Paul gave to regulate the use of spiritual gifts at Corinth in 1 Cor. 14.

9. Do we need miraculous powers to do the work of God today? Why do we sometimes think it would solve our problems to have such gifts? What does the Bible say?

10. Why did God remove supernatural gifts from the ongoing life of the church?

11/ Must We Believe in the Resurrection?

1 Cor. 15:1-58

Many men have died on crosses. In 519 B.C. the Persian King Darius crucified 3,000 Babylonians. In A.D. 66 the Romans crucified 3,600 Jews and thereby lit a flame of revolt which engulfed Palestine; by the time order was restored, the executioners had run out of wood for crosses.

It is not merely that Jesus of Nazareth died by crucifixion which makes people look to him for salvation. It is that he and the New Testament writers have made such *fantastic claims* for his death and that those claims have been *validated by his bodily resurrection.*

Jesus' own claim that he would rise from the dead was well-attested prior to his death. "From that time began Jesus to show unto his disciples, that he must go unto Jerusalem, and suffer many things of the elders and chief priests and scribes, and be killed, and the third day be raised up" (Matt. 16:21; cf. Mark 9:9; Luke 9:22; John 2:19). Even his enemies told Pilate, "Sir, we remember that that deceiver said while he was yet alive, After three days I rise again" (Matt. 27:63).

According to Jesus, the resurrection would be the single most definitive sign to mankind about his identity and role. "Then certain of the scribes and Pharisees answered him, saying, Teacher, we would see a sign from thee. But he answered and said unto them, An evil and adulterous generation seeketh after a sign; and there shall no sign be given to it but the sign of Jonah the prophet: for as Jonah was three days and three nights in the belly of the whale; so shall the Son of man be three days and three nights in the heart of the earth" (Matt. 12:38-40).

The ministry of Jesus would have ended, his claims would have been ignored, he would have been merely another martyr to religious rivalry, he would have been forgotten long ago – except for his resurrection.

The resurrection is claimed to have been an historical fact and is therefore subject to historical investigation. Either he rose from Joseph's new tomb, or he did not. Either our faith is genuine, or we engage in foolish self-delusion.

It was important for Paul to deal with the question of the resurrection – both Jesus' and our own – for the sake of the church at Corinth. The doctrine is central to the Christian religion. Paul himself said that the totality of the gospel message hinges on the truth or falsity of the bodily resurrection of Jesus (15:12-19).

The Gospel Account

These facts are admitted by everyone: Jesus died by crucifixion (Matt. 27:50; cf. John 19:31-35), he was buried in a nearby tomb provided by Joseph of Arimathea (Matt. 27:57-61), the tomb was sealed and a guard posted (Matt. 27:62-66), and *three days later the tomb was empty.*

How did the tomb come to be empty? It is here that the answers vary. The explanation offered by the guards responsible for protecting the tomb was this: "His disciples came by night, and stole him away while we slept" (Matt. 28:13). The account given by his disciples ran this way: "This Jesus did God raise up, whereof we all are witnesses" (Acts 2:32).

Was the body stolen?

If so, surely not by the Jewish or Roman officials connected with the proceedings. They had taken care to seal the tomb against the possibility of such a theft. If they had decided to remove the body to some secret burial place for safekeeping, they could have produced it later to quell the preaching of a bodily resurrection by his disciples.

If so, surely not by the disciples. When Jesus was arrested several hours before his death, "all the disciples left him, and fled" (Matt. 26:56). Peter denied him, Judas committed suicide, John came to the site of the cross, and the remainder evidently cowered in fear. This group was not of the temperament to challenge the authorities for the body of Jesus; they were more interested in saving their own necks. As one apostle later admitted, they did not understand – and therefore did not expect – a bodily resurrection at that point (John 20:9).

The soldiers' story that the disciples stole the body is not particularly credible. What court accepts the testimony of people concerning what happened while they were asleep? Could a group of soldiers sleep so soundly that the disciples could roll away a huge stone, remove the corpse, and leave without rousing even one?

Did the body rise from the dead?

There is consistent testimony to that effect from several good sources. Women (Matt. 28:1-10), individuals (Luke 24:34), groups (John 20:26-29) – masses of people affirmed that they saw him alive again. At least ten separate instances of such appearances are related in the New Testament. It is generally conceded that these people were honest, in position to know the facts of the matter, and had nothing to gain and much to lose in telling a lie. These people exhibited personal devotion to Christ on the basis of the resurrection, and many of them died for their faith rather than recant it as false.

The first public claims of a resurrection were made in the same city where it allegedly happened and where they would have been exposed if untrue.

The establishment and spread of the church is directly traceable to the doctrine of the resurrection. That all the things recorded in Acts could have been accomplished on the foundation of a falsehood would be a greater miracle than the bodily resurrection!

The Facts and the Faith

A century ago, Lord Lyttleton and Gilbert West set about to discredit Christianity by disproving Paul's conversion and Christ's resurrection. After examining the facts, both these men confessed their faith in Jesus! As Lyttleton realized, the most ardent persecutor of the church would have required a personal confrontation with the resurrected Christ in order to be turned from his hatred for and opposition to him (Acts 9:1-22; 22:6-21; 26:4-23).

How ironic that the most extended discussion of the doctrine of Christ's resurrection and its implications for our own would come from the pen of a man who once ridiculed the claim

What Is At Stake? (15:1-19)

Paul reminded the Corinthians that the doctrine of the resurrection is at the heart of the gospel he had preached among them and they had received and believed (15:1). His concern for them was that they "hold fast the word" and prove that they had not believed "in vain" (i.e., Gr, *eikē* = rashly, without due consideration, cf. Matt. 13:21).

The preaching of the gospel revolves around the fact that "Christ died for our sins according to the scriptures; and that he was buried; and that he hath been raised on the third day according to the scriptures" (15:3b-4). The *gospel* (i.e., good news) is not a set of behavioral responses imposed on us by a superior power. It is a message of love, grace, peace. By means of the death, burial, and resurrection of Christ, God is wooing and winning hearts by the lengths to which he has gone for our sakes. He allowed us to push him around, abuse him, and drive him to a cross. There he defeats us at last – not by his power but by his unconquerable weakness (cf. 1 Cor. 1:25b).

This doctrine of a resurrection-validated atonement is "of first importance" to Christianity (15:3a RSV).

In emphasizing that the death, burial, and resurrection occurred "according to the scriptures," Paul was appealing to Old Testament prophecies concerning the event (cf. Luke 24:44-46). Although he does not cite particular passages, we could consult any number from our own knowledge of Scripture. Both Paul (Acts 13:35) and Peter (Acts 2:25-28) preached Christ's resurrection from Psalm 16. Isaiah 53 was probably the favorite preaching text of the early Christian evangelists (cf. Acts 8:32ff).

Besides Old Testament predictions, Paul also cited numerous eyewitness reports of the resurrection – including his own (15:4-8). We would like to have more details about some of these appearances of Christ. In Paul's own day, however, these accounts were apparently widely circulated and well-known. In mentioning the appearance to "above five hundred brethren at once, of whom the greater part remain until now," there is an implied challenge to the Corinthians that they could consult and check the stories of these men at their discretion.

In beautiful humility, Paul comments on his own experience of the risen Christ (15:9-10). He did not deserve that vision of the exalted Son of God. It was a matter of divine grace shown to him, and that grace had both enabled and inspired him to serve Christ. He and his fellow apostles preached the same gospel with equal emphasis on the centrality of the resurrection: "Whether then it be I or they, so we preach, and so ye believed" (15:11).

Some at Corinth were denying a general resurrection of all the dead. Paul insisted that such a doctrine was inconsistent with the gospel he had preached at Corinth and which they had believed. "Now if Christ is preached that he hath been raised from the dead, how say some among you that there is no resurrection of the dead?" (15:12).

The reasoning here is extremely precise in logical terms. Paul's thesis in preaching the gospel at Corinth was clearly this: *Since Christ has been raised from the dead, all men will be raised and brought to Judgment* (cf. Acts 17:31). By affirming the antecedent (i.e., Christ has been raised from the dead), one was committed to the consequent (i.e., all men will be raised and brought to Judgment). On the other hand, by denying the consequent (i.e., all men will be raised and brought to Judgment), one implied a denial of the antecedent (i.e., Christ has been raised from the dead). As with logical entailments today, men do not always realize what is involved in some positions they embrace. Paul traced them out for his readers in the hope that it would shock them into rejecting such a view.

If there is no general resurrection, the following things must follow: (1) Christ himself has not really been raised (15:13); (2) preaching and faith focused on him are vain (15:14), (3) Paul and the other apostles were bearing false testimony about the workings of God (15:15-16).

While tracing out logical implications of positions, Paul proceeded to show what was entailed in a denial of Christ's personal resurrection: (1) the faith of the saints at Corinth was "vain" and had not delivered them from sin (15:17); (2) deceased Christians have simply perished, for they have no hope of being raised from their graves (15:18); (3) anything one was enduring for the sake of Christ was a foolish waste and left him deserving nothing more than pity (15:19).

What a powerful indictment of any position which denies either Christ's personal resurrection or a general resurrection of all the dead! Would the Corinthians be horrified to see what this false doctrine being taught by some really meant? Paul hoped so. He wanted them to recoil from a doctrine which would emasculate the entire gospel message.

He Arose! (15:20-34)

Against the denial of the resurrection by some, Paul proceeds to affirm the doctrine with bold assurance: "But Christ has indeed been raised from the dead, the firstfruits of those who have fallen asleep" (15:20). Yes, Christ has been raised! This doctrine is at the heart of the gospel you have embraced! More than that, it is the promise (i.e., firstfruits = a sacrifice at the start of harvest and a pledge of the remainder) of your own victory over death!

Christians know that death became the common fate of all humans through the sin of Adam. We have now been assured that resurrection from the grave will be the shared fate of all through the resurrection of Christ (15:22-23). Then, at the second coming of Christ, "the end" will be written to the drama of human activity on planet earth. The curtain will come down on history as Christ's final enemy (i.e., death) is destroyed and the kingdom is delivered up to the Father's sovereignty (15:24-28).

Then comes what many think is the most obscure and difficult verse in the entire Bible: "Else what shall they do that are baptized for the dead? If the dead are not raised at all, why then are they baptized for them?" (15:29). Were the Corinthians practicing some sort of vicarious baptism on behalf of people who had died unimmersed? It is not inconceivable, although we have no historical evidence of such a practice in the first century. It would seem strange for Paul to refer to such a custom without denouncing it, for it stands against everything that signifies personal responsibility in salvation. Were some of the Corinthians baptized with a view toward being reunited with their dead Christian friends in a future life? This view is more plausible than the previous one, yet it requires an unusual understanding of the Greek preposition *huper* (i.e., on behalf of). Was Paul making some obscure reference to the baptism which now-deceased Christians had received in hope of their future resurrection and participation in Christ's glory? This interpretation avoids the superstitious business of proxy baptism but is not without the difficulty of sounding strained. We must admit that it is beyond our ability to formulate a definitive interpretation of the verse.

Although we do not know what being "baptized for the dead" refers to, we can know the significance of it to Paul's argument. If there is no resurrection, nothing we do on behalf of the dead or to overcome death is of value. All such deeds are meaningless if there is no life to follow this one.

In his own experience, why should Paul subject himself to dangers for the sake of the gospel, if there is no resurrection? (15:30). Why carry the burden of daily ministry for the church? (15:31). Why fight with beasts – whether literal or figurative – for the sake of a faith which cannot conquer death? (15:32a). In fact, if Christianity has no sure hope of a future life, we would be better advised to live by the pagan motto "Let us eat and drink, for tomorrow we die" (15:32b).

Too much is at stake in this doctrine of the resurrection. Thus Paul counsels those who share his hope to avoid the corrupting company of those who deny the resurrection (15:33) and thus to avoid their sin of false teaching (15:34).

The Body We Will Have (15:35-58)

Every preacher has been asked the question Paul anticipated in verse 35: "How are the dead raised? With what kind of body will they come?" (NIV). What of a cremated body? What about someone buried at sea? Questions of this sort seem to be without end.

Paul responded: "How foolish! What you sow does not come to life unless it dies" (15:36). The charge of "foolishness" was evidently a rebuke to those at Corinth who thought themselves so wise in spiritual matters (cf. 1 Cor. 8:1). People of such insight should have been able to discern the answer to this question from events in nature! Several analogies are then presented to illustrate the method of the resurrection.

First, the seed analogy (15:37-38) teaches that the new body will be related to and in some ways similar to the seed from which it comes.

Second, the different flesh analogy (15:39) teaches that each creature has a body appropriate to its nature and environment.

Third, the heavenly bodies analogy (15:40-41) teaches that God gives all things in creation a body which reflects the proper "glory" of its estate.

"So also is the resurrection of the dead. It is sown

in corruption; it is raised in incorruption: it is sown in dishonor; it is raised in glory: it is sown in weakness; it is raised in power: it is sown a natural body; it is raised a spiritual body. If there is a natural body, there is also a spiritual body" (15:42-44). All this amounts to saying that our resurrection bodies will be like Christ's resurrection body. It will be substantive in nature (i.e., not a ghostly and disembodied form), recognizable, and personal – though more glorious than in its present mortal form. It will not be subject to decay or death. It will be "immortal" in nature. Just as surely as we have borne the natural form of bodies made from and for this earth, so shall we surely bear the glorious form of one like Christ's post-resurrection body (15:45-49).

In fact, such a change in bodily form is necessary to share in the eternal kingdom of God. "I declare to you, brothers, that flesh and blood cannot inherit the kingdom of God, nor does the perishable inherit the imperishable. Listen, I tell you a mystery: We shall not all sleep, but we shall all be changed – in a flash, in the twinkling of an eye, at the last trumpet. For the trumpet will sound, the dead will be raised imperishable, and we shall be changed. For the perishable must clothe itself with the imperishable, and the mortal with immortality" (15:50-53 NIV).

Whether one dies before the Lord returns or is alive at his coming, his or her earthly body will have to changed into the form which is appropriate for a never-ending existence. God is concerned about and involved with our lives now. But his ultimate goal for believers is to bring us to glory and immortality in heaven. Then and only then will his purpose for our redemption be fully realized.

When all this is accomplished, death shall have been defeated (15:54; cf. Isa. 25:8). Death will have neither "victory" nor "sting" (15:55; cf. Hos. 13:14) any more.

Death is the last enemy of Christ and his redemptive work (cf. 15:26). For the moment, it still reigns. It reigns only because its sting (i.e., its power to inflict harm) is potent. "The sting of death is sin; and the power of sin is the law" (15:56). Sin is the cause of death, and the occasion of sin is our failure in relation to divine law.

This takes us right back to the opening lines of the chapter: The *gospel* (i.e., good news) is that God has taken the demand laid on us and has fulfilled it through the sacrifice of his Son! (Rom. 5:8). We could not satisfy a perfect law with perfect obedience. Jesus honored the law of God with perfect obedience on our behalf and has made his obedience a free gift to us! (2 Cor. 5:21).

The ultimate offense against God – at Corinth or in our present situation at a much later point in history – is in being blind to our impotence, lostness, and hopelessness. So many at Corinth were in that condition. Thus the church was filled with problems. But when our helplessness apart from Christ is acknowledged, we recognize – with the publicans and sinners – that God's mercy has reached for us to redeem us, has offered to give us what we could never have achieved.

Redemption through Christ is validated through the resurrection. That wonderful event declared Jesus to be the Son of God and identified him as the only one under heaven in whom sinners can be set free from sin and death. Further, his resurrection is the guarantee of our own. We will be raised to share his glory!

What is the believer's response to all this? "Wherefore, my beloved brethren, be ye stedfast, unmovable, always abounding in the work of the Lord, forasmuch as ye know that your labor is not vain in the Lord" (1 Cor. 15:57-58). If Christ is not raised, all is "vain" and meaningless (cf. 15:14). Because he has been raised, we can labor abundantly – out of gratitude for his grace (cf. 15:10) – in the certain knowledge that we are victors!

The Difference It Makes

There is no such thing as an anti-supernatural form of Christianity. A good man who teaches inspiring lessons to humble followers has no claim to messiahship or deity apart from the *mighty works* and *signs* which have traditionally been used to authenticate heaven's agents on earth. Moses was allowed to work signs before Pharaoh; Elijah was vindicated by supernatural fire on Mt. Carmel; Daniel and his associates were delivered by God's mighty hand in their time of stress in Babylon. Would heaven send one of its own without credentials of supernatural power?

Nicodemus drew the correct conclusion from the miracles Jesus worked: "Rabbi, we know you are a teacher who has come from God. For no one could perform the miraculous signs you are doing if God were not with him" (John 3:2). The signs were heaven's stamp of approval on the claims Jesus was making for himself.

Above all other signs, however, stands the resurrection. On Pentecost, Peter appealed to three proofs of the deity and messiahship of Jesus – Old Testament prophecies, miracles worked by Jesus among the people, and the resurrection. In Athens, Paul said the resurrection was proof to all men of the truth of the Christian message. Can we say less?

We must not blush to declare and defend the doctrine which was made the foundation of New Testament Christianity. If we want to restore that faith to a world that is in such desperate need, we will have to give more than platitudes and expressions of concern. We must offer a redeeming Savior!

On the basis of the resurrection of Christ, we can proclaim him to be the Son of God (Matt. 12:38-40). We can say that his death was effective as an atonement for the sins of the whole race (Rom. 4:25). We can press for people to obey him in repentance and baptism in his name (Acts 2:38). We can preach the resurrection of all men from the dead and the certainty of Judgment before his throne (Heb. 9:27).

Conclusion

Does the resurrection matter? If one does not accept it, he can neither *believe in* nor *live by* the tenets of Christianity. In other words, this issue was not divorced from the moral and practical problems at Corinth. They went hand in hand.

Unable to believe any more in the general bodily resurrection of the dead, some at Corinth could no longer accept the gospel claim about Jesus' resurrection "according to the scriptures." Unable at that point to put themselves under the Lordship of Jesus, their lives were degenerating into a pattern hardly distinguishable from that of their pre-Christian days. A sound faith and a righteous life go hand in hand!

Yes, the doctrine of the bodily resurrection mattered at Corinth in the first century. It matters still and must remain at the heart of our proclamation of Jesus.

Study Questions

1. Demonstrate that Jesus anticipated his own resurrection and that this doctrine was not an afterthought by followers trying to put back together their messianic hope after the Savior's death.

2. Summarize the points of agreement about the death of Christ.

3. What are the differing explanations for the empty

tomb on the third day following his death? Evaluate the evidence for each position.

4. What was Paul's view of the centrality of the resurrection to Christian faith? What did he mean by saying that the doctrine is "of first importance"?

5. From this chapter and additional research, compile a full list of the post-resurrection appearances of Jesus.

6. Do people always understand the logical implications of positions they embrace? That is, do we always understand where a certain view will lead when we commit to it? How did Paul use this fact to try to shake the Corinthians loose from the false view of the resurrection some had taken in that church?

7. 1 Cor. 15:29 is a most difficult verse. Do some research on it. Can you form an opinion as to its meaning?

8. What are some of the questions you have wondered about concerning the bodies we will have in the resurrection? What insights do you get from Paul's discussion in 1 Cor. 15 that help answer those questions?

9. How did Nicodemus interpret the meaning of miracles and signs in Jesus' life? Was he correct? What does the resurrection of Jesus mean to the legitimacy of Christian faith?

10. Why are some hesitant to focus attention on the doctrine of the resurrection today? Do you think our generation is any more skeptical of the resurrection claim that people were in the first century? What difference might it make to our evangelistic efforts to begin with the bold confidence in Christ those earliest evangelists showed?

12/ A Final Word – And Farewell

1 Cor. 16:1-24

How would you close a letter to Corinth?

It was a troubled and struggling church. There were doctrinal problems and glaring moral failures. This was Paul's second piece of correspondence which had addressed their problems. To this point, there had been precious little – if any – evidence of progress among them.

Might you be tempted to close with scoldings and ringing threats? Would you set a time limit for the correction of the problems you had identified and addressed? Perhaps you would simply close on a note of terse formality and allow them to draw the conclusion that you were growing impatient with their worldly attitudes and ungodly behavior.

Here is how Paul closed: He encouraged them in a good work he knew they were helping with, expressed the desire to see them soon, and sent warm greetings to his beloved brethren.

Concern for the Poor

Having just concluded his extended discussion of the resurrection, Paul makes an immediate transition to the subject of a collection for the needy saints in Jerusalem. He was always concerned with both *doctrine* and *personal human need* among people his ministry touched. We need the same balance in our lives and ministries.

The early ideal of "ministry" held before me was long hours in the study, isolated from the distractions of phone calls, counseling, and one-on-one involvement with people. After all, the classes and sermons had to be first quality come Sunday morning! Unfortunately, many of those classes and sermons were sterile and without profit to their hearers. Oh, they were doctrinally sound. But they lacked the credibility that comes only of caring involvement in the lives of the people who heard them.

Paul was wiser. Without neglecting doctrine or failing to give carefully reasoned answers to difficult theological questions, he was sensitive to the personal dimensions of the message he preached. He understood that the foundation of Christianity is *love,* and love always shows itself in practical ways for the benefit of others.

The Collection (16:1)

The formula "now concerning" introduces the final in a series of questions dealt with in the second half of the book. The previous ones have been about marriage (7:1-40), meat sacrificed to idols (8:1 – 11:1), worship (11:2-34), spiritual gifts (12:1 – 14:40), and the resurrection of the body (15:1-58). This one has to do with a collection of funds for some unfortunate brethren in Judea.

Acts mentions a famine which came over the Roman Empire during the reign of Claudius, A.D. 41-54 (Acts 11:28). The full force of it apparently hit around A.D. 45 or shortly thereafter; it is not inconceivable that some were still suffering from its effects almost a decade later. From the base of work among the Gentiles in Antioch of Syria, a collection was taken among non-Jewish Christians to help relieve their needs and to demonstrate the oneness of the body of Christ (Acts 11:29-30). The collection mentioned here (and later in 2 Cor. 8 – 9) is probably a continuation of that ministry.

The instructions about to be given to Corinth were the same Paul had already given to the churches of Galatia – and presumably other pre-dominantly Gentile churches. Over the centuries, the guidelines for this contribution have been taken as the basic pattern for the way Christians should give to the work of the church both in times of crisis and for "routine maintenance" of her ongoing ministries.

Setting Aside Funds (16:2-4)

The regular meeting day for Christians at Je-rusalem, Corinth, and throughout the Roman Em-pire was "the first day of the week" (16:2a). Literally, the Greek text uses an expression which should be translated "on the first day of *every* week" (cf. NIV). As the church met Sunday after Sunday, the saints were to be collecting their gifts together on a reg-ular and systematic basis.

Paul wanted every believer to participate (i.e., "each one of you") at a level which was proportion-ate to his ability (i.e., "as he may prosper"). The gift was thus being collected not as a tax or by any fixed and assigned amount but as a freewill offering.

Although some commentators understand Paul's instruction "lay by him in store" (16:2b) to refer to separate funds being kept in the homes of individ-ual believers (e.g., Chrysostom, Robertson and Plummer, Bruce), such a procedure would defeat

Paul's express purpose of avoiding having to gather the funds together when he arrived (i.e., "that no collections be made when I come"). It seems more likely that he is referring to what we have come to call "the church treasury."

Paul also hoped that someone representing the Corinthian church could accompany the funds to Jerusalem (16:3). The purpose for this was apparently to allow each participating congregation to see that the money was used properly and to avoid any suspicion of wrongdoing among those collecting and handling it (cf. 2 Cor. 6:16-21). The apostle himself hoped to travel with the group and to visit Jerusalem again in connection with the gift (16:4).

Some Personal Matters

A Projected Visit (16:5-9)

Although his plans were not rigid, he hoped to come to Corinth later in the year (A.D. 55) and spend the winter with the brethren there (16:5-7). Although Paul sometimes had to change his plans due to unforeseen circumstances, he appears to have made the visit talked about here.

From the record of Paul's travels given in Acts, we learn that he left Ephesus (i.e., the place from which he wrote 1 Cor.), visited Macedonia, and then spent three months in Greece. "And after the uproar ceased, Paul having sent for the disciples and exhorted them, took leave of them, and departed to go into Macedonia. And when he had gone through those parts, and had given them much exhortation, he came into Greece. And when he had spent three months there, and a plot was laid against him by the Jews as he was about to set sail for Syria, he determined to return through Macedonia" (Acts 20:1-3).

The three-month winter spent at Corinth would

have allowed him to deal with some of the problems raised in the letter.

The reason for his delay from spring to winter before coming to Corinth was the fruitful ministry which was currently in progress at Ephesus. "But I will tarry at Ephesus until Pentecost; for a great door and effectual door is opened unto me, and there are many adversaries" (16:8-9).

Ephesus was the most important city in the Roman province of Asia. The Temple of Artemis (Diana) dominated it and was one of the wonders of the ancient world. Paul brought the gospel to that city on his second missionary tour (Acts 18:18-19) and returned there for an extended work during his third journey (Acts 19:8-10). He worked "special miracles" (Acts 19:11-12), and his preaching generated a phenomenal response (Acts 19:20).

Eventually, however, the guild of silversmiths who made a living in connection with the worship of Artemis generated a riot against Paul (Acts 19:23ff). So his report to the Corinthians was precisely correct: there was a great door of evangelistic opportunity at Ephesus, but there was also determined opposition.

His Co-Workers (16:10-12)

While still at Ephesus, Paul sent Timothy to Corinth to give attention to the things troubling the church (Acts 19:22). Knowing that there was some opposition growing to his own work, he feared Timothy might receive a rude reception. He wanted them to receive him warmly (16:10) and without intimidating him (16:11a; cf. 1 Tim. 4:12). More than that, he wanted them to encourage him and "set him forward on his journey with peace" (16:11b).

Some at Corinth were hoping that Apollos would return. One would assume that the party of people wearing his name was especially eager in this behalf. Although Paul had encouraged him to go there, he had refused (16:12). He may have been busy with other works; he may have wanted to avoid fueling the personal loyalties some were promoting around his name.

Closing the Epistle

The final general exhortation of the book is given at this point: "Be on your guard; stand firm in the faith; be men of courage; be strong. Do everything in love" (16:13-14 NIV).

Each element of this exhortation is particularly appropriate in calling to mind the central themes of the epistle. "Be on your guard" – against falling into sin because of your arrogance (cf. 1 Cor. 10:12). "Stand firm in the faith" – focusing on the Lord Jesus rather than on his human messengers (cf. 1 Cor. 1:10 – 4:21). "Be men of courage" – acting as adults and mature believers rather than children (cf. 1 Cor. 3:1-3). "Be strong" – for spiritual sickness and weakness are threatening death to some saints at Corinth (cf. 1 Cor. 11:30).

"Do everything in love." It was their lack of love which was at the root of their spiritual impotence. They were empowered with spiritual gifts, but they could not use them profitably because of rivalry and jealousy. Exercising gifts, teaching the gospel, disciplining an impenitent brother, dealing with marriages in jeopardy – everything at Corinth had to be done within the scope of Christian *agapē* (cf. 1 Cor. 13; 16:24).

Paul encouraged the whole church to look to the example of dedicated service being set by the family of Stephanus and to imitate it (16:15-16). Stephanus and the two other brothers named (16:17-18) were probably the bearers of the letter containing the questions submitted to the apostle from Corinth.

Greetings were forwarded to Corinth from "the

churches of Asia" (i.e., Ephesus and her sister churches), Aquila and Priscilla, and "all the brethren" associated with Paul (16:19-20). Adding his handwritten authentication to the letter is characteristic of Paul (16:21). God's grace (16:23) and his personal love for the saints (16:24) are the closing benedictions.

Most interesting of all in these closing lines is verse 22: "If any man loveth not the Lord, let him be anathema. Maran-atha." To pronounce an "anathema" on an individual is to invoke God's curse on him. Paul speaks so harshly only in relation to the man whose heart is corrupt. Some at Corinth were immoral, and others were doctrinally unsound. The whole church was caught up in personality cults and division. There is no general anathema on the whole congregation, however. Even with their problems, Paul granted that the Corinthians loved the Lord. He evidently believed that God's grace could bear with them through their struggles and that he should bear with them, too.

Depending on the way the word is divided (i.e., *Maran-atha* or *Marana-tha*), the final part of the verse is something like a prayer or greeting which must have been common among the earliest Christians. It is an Aramaic word which has been transliterated into Greek. Divided in the former manner, it would mean "Our Lord has come." The latter division would make it the more emphatic "Our Lord, come!"

Conclusion

Throughout the epistle, Paul has been loyal to Christ and uncompromising with the truth. His dream was that every believer should come to love Christ and fill his heart with the truth for the sake of spiritual maturity. Yet his charges at Corinth were far from the ideal.

Thus, throughout the epistle, he has been gracious and loving. He has practiced love's essence in believing the best about the Corinthians – assured that they loved Christ and wanted to do what was right. They were still "the church of God at Corinth." They were still God's family, heaven's vineyard, and Paul's brothers and sisters.

It is a delicate and difficult balance to maintain. Love the truth, but love the brethren who are following it imperfectly! Love the struggling and weak child of God, but do not compromise the holy demands of truth and righteousness for the sake of corrupted sympathies! Paul did a better job of keeping these two concerns in proper tension than some others of us do. His example is worth studying and imitating.

That church at Corinth was worth caring about, praying for, and building up. It was like the church where I am a member. It might even remind you of the one where you are.

The Lord doesn't have any perfect churches. So don't be so discouraged. Don't quit. Don't give up. Keep on caring, praying, and building!

We are imperfect people in imperfect churches who serve a Perfect Savior. Our hope lies not with ourselves – but in Him!

Study Questions

1. Is there anything surprising about the way Paul ends this epistle? Is this a change in manner from the way the earlier part of the letter has run?

2. The importance of "balance" is discussed early in this chapter. How did Paul balance *doctrine* and *personal human need* in his ministry among the Corinthians? Do we tend to do as well?

3. What was the background to the collection of funds Paul was taking up among the Gentile churches of the empire?

4. What was the special meeting day of the early

church? How often did they assemble on that day? What
was the purpose of those assemblies?

5. From the information given in Acts, trace the movements of Paul from the time of writing this epistle through
the writing of the letter we call 2 Cor.

6. What did Paul mean by an "open door" being provided him at Ephesus? What was the nature of the opposition to his ministry there?

7. How did Timothy fit into Paul's immediate plans
for the sake of helping the church at Corinth? What did
he ask of the Corinthians for Timothy's sake?

8. Reflect carefully on each part of the closing exhortation of this epistle at 1 Cor. 16:13-14.

9. Discuss 1 Cor. 16:22 at some length.

10. What lesson from this epistle has been most meaningful to you? How do you plan to implement that lesson
in your life? In the life of the church where you are?

Bibliography

Barrett, C. K. *A Commentary on the First Epistle to the Corinthians*. Harper's New Testament Commentaries. New York: Harper & Row, Publishers, 1968.

Barrett, C. K. *Essays on Paul*. Philadelphia: The Westminster Press, 1982.

Bauer, Walter. *A Greek-English Lexicon of the New Testament and Other Early Christian Literature,* 2nd ed. Translated and augmented by William F. Arndt, F. Wilbur Gingrich, and Frederick W. Danker. Chicago: University of Chicago Press, 1979.

Bruce, F. F. *1 & 2 Corinthians*. New Century Bible Commentary. Grand Rapids: Wm. B. Eerdmans Publ. Co., 1971.

142

Buttrick, George Arthur, ed. *The Interpreter's Bible*. 12 vols. New York: Abingdon Press, 1953. Vol. 10: *The First Epistle to the Corinthians,* by Clarence Tucker Craig.

Holladay, Carl. *The First Letter of Paul to the Corinthians*. Living Word Commentary. Austin, TX: Sweet Publishing Company, 1979.

International Standard Bible Encyclopedia, 1979 ed. S.v. "Corinth," by D. H. Madvig.

International Standard Bible Encyclopedia, 1979 ed. S.v. "Corinthians, First Epistle to the," by Leon Morris.

Gaebelein, Frank E., gen. ed. *Expositor's Bible Commentary*. 12 vols. Grand Rapids: Zondervan Publishing House, 1976. Vol. 10: *1 Corinthians,* by W. Harold Mare.

Robertson, Archibald, and Plummer, Alfred. *A Critical and Exegetical Commentary on the First Epistle of St Paul to the Corinthians,* 2nd ed. International Critical Commentary. Edinburgh: T. & T. Clark, 1914.

Additional Study Books
By Rubel Shelly

A Book-By-Book Study of the Old Testament

A Book-By-Book Study of the New Testament

Happiness Is...
(Studies in the Beatitudes)

What Christian Living is All About
(Studies in James)

Something to Hold Onto
(Studies in 1 & 2 Peter)

The Lamb and His Enemies
(Studies in Revelation)

Going On To Maturity
(Steps in Spiritual Growth)